# HOW TO SPEAK HUMAN

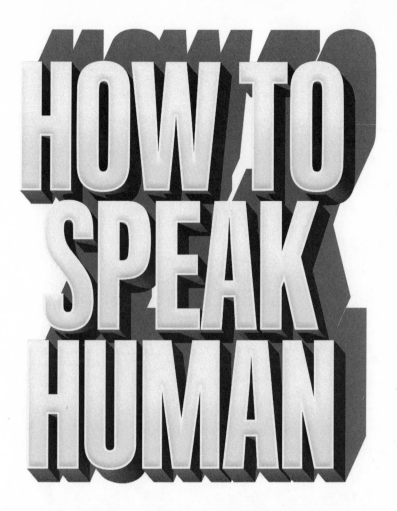

# HOW TO SPEAK HUMAN

## A practical guide to getting the best from the humans you work with

**JACKSON** & **JACKSON**

From award-winning employee experience company, Jaxzyn.

# WILEY

First published in 2018 by John Wiley & Sons Australia, Ltd
42 McDougall St, Milton Qld 4064

Office also in Melbourne

Typeset in 11.5/13.5 pt Adobe Garamond Pro

© John Wiley & Sons Australia, Ltd 2018

The moral rights of the authors have been asserted

A catalogue record for this book is available from the National Library of Australia

Cover design by Jaxzyn

Cover typography by Luke Lucas

Internal illustrations by Barry Patenaude

Printed in Singapore by C.O.S. Printers Pte Ltd

10 9 8 7 6 5 3 2 1

**Disclaimer**

The material in this publication is of the nature of general comment only, and does not represent professional advice. It is not intended to provide specific guidance for particular circumstances and it should not be relied on as the basis for any decision to take action or not take action on any matter which it covers. Readers should obtain professional advice where appropriate, before making any such decision. To the maximum extent permitted by law, the authors and publisher disclaim all responsibility and liability to any person, arising directly or indirectly from any person taking or not taking action based on the information in this publication.

*For M.L.T.*
*One of our favourite humans, who taught us the value of words.*

# Contents

*About the authors*     *ix*

*Hoisting the banner for human*     *xiii*

*How to speak human*     *xxiii*

*How to speak whaaat?*     *xxix*

**Curiosity** The insatiable hunger of a curious mind     1

**Anticipation** The exquisite agony of anticipation     17

**Surprise!** The unanticipated delight of the unexpected     27

**Visual** The sensory superiority of visual     41

👀 **Beware** ... The insidious fog of habituation     57

**Narratives** The titillations of a well-told tale     65

**Emotions** The paradoxical logic of getting emotional     77

**Humour** The serious business of being funny     87

👀 **Caution** ... The complication of complexity     95

**Words** The power of using and choosing words wisely     107

**Names** The undeniable sweetness of a well-chosen name     117

**Language** The power of language to shift perception     127

**Modes** The perks of matching the mode to the message     149

👀 **Beware** ... The excuses for mediocrity     167

*Time, tide and the inevitability of change*     *177*

*So* ...     *181*

*Acknowledgements*     *183*

*Index*     *185*

# About the authors

Dougal and Jen Jackson are a couple of curious humans with a fascination for what makes people tick. Founders of employee experience company Jaxzyn, they consider themselves mighty fortunate to work with a diverse team of thinkers, communicators, creators and doers, discovering and implementing ways to make our workplaces more human.

Jaxzyn is a small company with a big vision: an unshakable belief that organisations *can* have it all. They can be profitable. They can be good for society and the environment. And they can be wonderful places to work, where people go to work happy and return home happier, better for having gone to work that day. Perhaps we're a little starry-eyed, but we'd rather be part of a world that believes that better is possible.

Along the way we've been privileged to work with like-minded folk from organisations such as PepsiCo, Mattel, Novartis, Amazon, Nestlé, Probuild, Origin Energy, Urban Utilities and Blue Care. It's these few — the difference-makers and visionaries, trendsetters and forward-thinkers, influencers and leaders — that move the many. These are the people who push departments, organisations and industries forward. People, just like you and just like us, who believe in possibility. Believe in *human*.

Dougal leads research and development at Jaxzyn. He spends his days researching, writing, making, thinking and surfing (and thinking *about* surfing). He draws on a background in design and communication to bring an unorthodox approach to a corporate landscape typically starved of creativity. Dougal holds an unwavering belief in the power of ideas, and human-centred design as a tool to connect with people at all levels of an organisation. You'll hear his voice in the flamboyant exposition and rumination that abound in this book.

Jen is head of strategy and business development at Jaxzyn. She spends her days chatting, caffeinating and strategising with co-conspirators (aka clients) from around the world. Making her way from farm to city, Jen champions humans of all stripes (and plaids). She has a unique ability to slice through layers of complexity, cut to the core of the matter and communicate with creative flair and dairy farmer simplicity. You'll hear her voice connecting the theory with real-world practical application.

And that's all you really need to know about us. There's more exciting topics ahead, so let's get on with it, shall we?

# Hoisting the banner for human

What a glorious age to be alive, mates.

Rapidly disappearing in the rear-view mirror are stiff, impersonal workplaces painted various shades of beige. Here and ahead lies a profound shift towards human, a fast-approaching future where people are celebrated. Not just customers or shareholders either, but the vast majority of folk inside our organisations—the people who keep things moving.

Sure, the rise of the Silicon Valley start-up scene brought office slippery slides, pinball machines and other wonders. But we're not talking about ball pits or other gimmickry. Peel back the layers and peer behind the superficial veneers; there's something far more real.

It's a restlessness, a discontent with old ways and outdated methods. After decades spent stripping all the human out of business, there's a movement towards putting it all back in.

Do we really need a book called *How to Speak Human* to help us, though?

Sure, it's a cute title—intended to twist mouths into wry smiles. But we can't be for real, can we? After all, we're all humans. And speaking is just a matter of opening our mouths and letting the words fall out. As natural as nudity in nature...

Yet somehow it isn't.

Somewhere along the way, amidst the busyness, the business, the technology and the professionalism, it became harder to connect with the people around us. Harder to speak human, to get attention, to influence, to engage.

For folk who've been thrust into leadership positions, connecting with people, despite technical skills and the best intentions, can seem like it requires a whole other language.

But the good news, friends, is that like French, German or Japanese—though not so much Latin (because that shit is complicated)—it's a language that can be taught. Heck, it's a language that's already in all of us, though often buried, like a shy tortoise that needs an encouraging finger to coax it from its shell. It's the language of human.

**Here and ahead lies a profound shift towards human, a fast-approaching future where people are celebrated.** So here we are. Smack bang in the middle of a movement driven by savvy folk (like you) to bring human back. These changes are happening right this moment, as we type, and as you read. But why *now*? What created this perfect climate for change...or the perfect storm for any organisation, leader or individual who doesn't keep pace?

## A paddle but no canoe

Only a few years ago it was pretty common for us to be working on five-, even ten-year strategies. But in the last couple of years it's more often 12-month roadmaps, with only the haziest vision for beyond. This parallels the rapidly changing nature of the world we live in, a time when we have only the slightest inkling of what might come next.

With industries seemingly being disrupted (excuse the buzzword) daily, our workplaces are volatile environments. From transport to communication to currency, like time, tide and taxes, change is our new constant. If we aren't dealing with it personally, we're guiding others through it. Then, just as we get it all figured out, everything turns downside-up.

With all this volatility comes a healthy amount of uncertainty. Where is our industry going? How do we stay relevant? How do we stay ahead? Will our role even exist in another 12 months? And what about artificial intelligence coming to steal our jobs?

These are complex questions, and unfortunately there's no certain answers to any of them, friends. We're adrift in ambiguity, with a set of oars and no canoe.

Volatility, uncertainty, complexity, ambiguity — this is the world we live in, and these the challenges we face daily. So much so that boffins have even given it a catchy, yet particularly wart-sounding acronym: VUCA.

The problem is that many organisations still move at a glacial pace. Taking six to nine months to approve a 12-month roadmap for distribution is the opposite of agile. Humans hardly respond well to change either. Of the ten most stressful life events (according to the Social Readjustment Rating Scale), all involve some type of change. Heck, some aren't even inherently negative (we're looking at you, marriage and retirement).

So it's also little wonder that the slightest sign of change at work causes people to behave like panicked beasts on castration day. Stressed and stampeding, snouts to the breeze, sensing blood. Not a healthy state for producing our best work.

If change is hard for most folk, it's particularly tough on leaders. It's difficult to speak in certainties when we feel like we're only a step or two ahead ourselves. It's challenging to chart a clear course of action for others when we're not entirely sure of what lies ahead.

Through uncertain and foggy seas ahead, mates, human is our beacon.

## Same same, but different

Cheetahs, leopards, jaguars, tigers and bobcats. Similarly: Traditionalists, Baby Boomers, Generation Xers, Generation Yers, and Generation Zers. Don't let appearances fool you. All are from the same family, but they're very different species.

A combination of living longer and working later means that for the first time it's not uncommon to share our workplace with five generations, each influenced by very different social, political and technological climates, with entirely different beliefs and expectations around what work should be.

These differences became blatantly obvious as Millennials began filling our workplaces. Oh, the uproar those upstarts caused! Growing up being told they could do, be and achieve anything, they approached work with an equal sense of possibility.

For younger generations, work is more than just a wage. There's an expectation that companies will provide purpose and progress. They want to work for brands they believe in, and to believe that their work contributes to something bigger than themselves or even the company. They want to know why they're doing what they're doing. There's an expectation of transparency.

For older generations who've weathered tougher times, banging away in undesirable jobs day in, day out, to support their families through times when simply having a job was considered fortunate, this attitude came across a lot like entitlement.

'We did it tough — they should suck it up.'

'Work is called "work" for a reason!'

But the times — and expectations — they are a-changin'. And the difference between resigned stoicism and naive entitlement is entirely a matter of perspective.

Then there's technology. While the older generations grew up in dark times before the internet (what did we even do back then?) and mobile devices, the younger generations have always been connected. Responding to messages seems perfectly natural, often to the disgruntlement of older generations that would never have considered taking a personal call at work.

Heck, the generations aren't our only divide. Technology and globalisation have meant many of us work with a massively diverse spectrum of humans from around the world. The disconnect between countries, cultures, departments, even between management and frontline roles, can be vast. It's not uncommon to feel like we're all speaking entirely different languages.

## Fainting goats and other whimsy

You needn't go much further than your social media feeds to see how humans communicate in our natural habitat.

Go on, take a peek at what thrills us, but we warn you—it sure ain't pretty. If ever there was evidence that humanity is not quite as evolved as we may like to think we are, social media will confirm it.

The facts? We communicate in machine-gun bursts and consume in bite-sized chunks. We text, tweet, message, comment and chat across multiple channels, platforms and devices, to multiple people—often at the same time. We share YouTube clips of cats being terrorised by cucumbers. We create ridiculous memes based on pop culture references, then we LOL about it.

We talk about topics that make us feel something: funny, sad, angry or confused. We curate the content that interests us and ruthlessly block any that doesn't. We're frequently exposed to language and grammar that slaps the hallowed *Oxford English Dictionary* right in the covers.

But here's the kicker.

Of the 7.6 billion humans currently spinning around on this planet, about 3 billion of us leave home with unbridled enthusiasm for full- or part-time jobs. Here, we—the same people who're amused by videos of goats fainting, who send messages composed of single emoticons, who spend evenings WhatsApping and Snapchatting—do things, make things, invent things, fix things and sell things.

And while we're all at work—doing things, making things, inventing things, fixing things and selling things—guess what changes in our communication preferences?

Nothing at all.

We remain amused by fainting goats. We continue to 😂 at our friends. We continue to communicate with each other exactly the way we did at home.

Meanwhile, any guesses how the companies we work for typically communicate with us?

Yep. A xeroxed memo on corporate letterhead — straight from nineteen-fifty-bloody-three.

Apparently there are more than a few in the corporate world who'd be fascinated to discover the sheer number of communication options available to humans as viable alternatives to Microsoft PowerPoint.

Texting, visual languages, emoji, memes — myriads of entirely new and emerging technologies creating entirely new ways to connect and communicate. It's enough to leave you speechless.

**The disconnect between countries, cultures, departments, even between management and frontline roles, can be vast. It's not uncommon to feel like we're all speaking entirely different languages.**

Yet of all the possibilities for communication, many businesses barely scratch the surface. Even the behemoths of the business world, brands you'd expect to be right on point, frequently use methods lagging years behind the world beyond their office walls.

## Weary old dinosaurs

Oh yes, everything has changed. Yet many organisations still have underpinning assumptions about people and efficiency that haven't changed since the industrial revolution.

Like a time capsule or Egyptian tomb, stepping into some established companies is like entering a lost world in a bygone era. Marvel at the archaic systems and processes! Wonder at their primitive beliefs! Take a deep breath of musty air, and do try to avoid the skeletons in the upper levels. I think they once called these architectural features 'the corner suite'.

We jest, of course.

The age of a business (or human) is by no means representative of their relevance or importance. However, age often equates to entrenched assumptions, made worse when they also happen to be old *and* large.

Small is agile, able to adjust course quickly with each gust or tiniest variation of the breeze. Larger is more cumbersome — the biggest ships are hardest to turn. The great leviathans of the business world chart courses with only a vague notion of what lies over the horizon, leaving them vulnerable to the slightest change of weather. The smallest change to their trajectory requires time, money and all hands on deck. It's no wonder they tend to just batten down the hatches and attempt to plough their way through.

Perhaps it's outdated beliefs that treat humans like resources. It may be communication techniques from a previous decade. It's the failure to consider the unique drivers and motivators that engage different segments of the workforce. It can be archaic, multilayered hierarchies or a lack of diversity in leadership teams (pale, stale and predominantly male!). It can be obsolete technology that frustrates rather than facilitates connection.

It's the companies most set in their ways that face the greatest challenges in the unpredictable times ahead.

## Nowhere to hide

Way back in 1998, while Tom Hanks was saving Private Ryan, McKinsey researchers declared that the most important resource for the next 20 years would be talent. They claimed that an organisation's success would depend on attracting, developing and retaining talented people.

And they were right.

Twenty years later, the *war for talent* is sounding a little long in the tooth, but the principles still hold true. Finding the right people isn't just smart—it's essential.

Making our courtship infinitely more difficult, though, is that we're savvier now than ever before. We live in an age of connection and transparency, where every hotel, flight, movie, meal and product can be selected based on peer reviews. So it's no surprise that when it comes to a decision as important as choosing where we'll spend the better part of our day, five days a week, we're just as diligent.

It's no longer enough to *claim* to be a great place to work; sites like Glassdoor are exposing the truth. With just a few clicks, we can find peer reviews that describe exactly what it's like to work for our potential employer. These aren't carefully manicured press releases by public relations; they are raw reviews about the experience, written by people just like us.

Employer branding has become a fundamental function. A choreographed mating dance to find the perfect people for our organisations. But wooing them isn't where the courtship ends. We need to keep them happy.

In late 2017, LinkedIn estimated that around 73 per cent of its 400(ish) million users were passive job seekers, open to jumping ship if the right opportunity came along. We're dealing with a workforce that has one eye on the exit, with plenty of options if we aren't treating them right.

## Rise of the robots

The people and businesses succeeding today and tomorrow are the ones keeping pace. But the ones who'll succeed in the future are already looking ahead ... to a time when many of our existing roles will be replaced by artificial intelligence.

Oh yes, the rise of the robots to take our jobs is as logical as it is inevitable.

Robots don't have short attention spans and aren't influenced by emotion. Robots don't have personal lives, or lives at all. Robots don't take lunch breaks. Robots are accurate and rarely make mistakes. Robots aren't concerned about the exploitation of robot labour. Robots do what they do without pay, and they do it unceasingly, unquestioningly, 24 hours a day, seven days a week.

An age of robots and AI-driven efficiency lies ahead of us, friends. But this doesn't mean we need to start speaking android. The new roles that will inevitably emerge will be more dependent on our relationships with each other.

Yes, our work will continue to rely on humans. Creatures comprising 60 per cent water and 40 per cent unfathomable thought processes, unreasonable behaviours and unpredictable emotions. Filled with all sorts of psychological and physiological inconveniences. Capable of equal parts frustration and—absolute delight.

# How to speak human

This book takes an unashamedly practical approach. A how-to that hurtles headlong and enthusiastically into the fascinations of science and theories of human communication. It draws on over a decade of working with savvy leaders from organisations around the world, penned with the hope that our experience might help you and others make a difference.

Along the way, we'll share the ways savvy folk (just like you) have brought these principles into their work to great effect. And, we'll suggest ideas for how you can apply them, right now, to whatever you're working on.

Our focus areas — attention, influence and engagement — come from the most common conversations we have every day.

*Attention* is about cutting through the noise and directing eyeballs exactly where we need them. It's essential for drawing awareness to new initiatives, and dragging people's focus back to important ongoing endeavours. It's an important precursor to engagement and a cognitive framer for learning.

*Influence* explores the human leadership skills we need to connect with people and teams. It's not about tricking or manipulating people into short-term change. No, we're talking about strategies that lead to enduring transformation and ensure great outcomes for everyone involved.

*Engagement* is right at the centre — the beating heart. It's a word often flung about by well-meaning HR professionals trying to measure an intangible. A two-point improvement on our engagement scores? High-bloody-fives! But this isn't about tools, diagnostics, metrics or measures. No, it's the practical things we can do every day to improve connection.

## A love song for engagement

Why aren't there happier ballads about business?

Countless lines have been sung about working-class men, working on weekends, working on railroads and chain gangs, working nine to five, and working hard all day well into the night, but nary a positive word for work amongst them.

There are plenty of positive tunes about love, fame, fortune, rolling through hoods with homies looking for honeys. Yet the seven dwarfs whistling their way down the mineshaft is one of the few to celebrate the brighter side of work.

This is a big chunk of our life we're talking about here. Where are the raps about ground-shaking presentations? Where are the electronic anthems about resolving all the IT issues? Where are the soaring orchestral paeans to visionary leaders?

If we were to write a song about business based on daily conversations with leaders, we'd call it 'Seeking Engagement'. We'd pen it as a love song, an acoustic ballad crooned wistfully by a jilted leader longing for their love to be reciprocated by an ambivalent workforce.

*Seeking engagement,*
*Just hoping for a little of your sweet engagement,*
*All alone and longing for the slightest sign you're engaged…*

Oh yes, it'd jerk tears right out of your eyeballs.

Perhaps the reason we have so few positive business melodies is that, according to global performance-management consultancy Gallup, ONLY 13 PER CENT OF THE GLOBAL BLOODY WORKFORCE ARE ENGAGED.

Chew on that statistic for a moment. That's over a billion people turning up to work with a vague sense of apathy and doing… well, pretty much the bare minimum. That's a lot of people going to work to gather inspiration for their next anti-work acoustic blues ditty.

Countless studies have proven the cost of low engagement. A quick jaunt through Google will provide you with pages of evidence, and just as many promises of magical solutions to all your engagement problems.

Roll up, roll up, and roll out the engagement survey! Behold the once-every-two-years opportunity to get to know your people. Marvel at our conjurer: wand in his left hand, top hat in his right, a collective gasp as he plucks the engagement score from within. Watch as the revelation sends our HR/People and Culture departments into a spin.

Yes, we've really begun to dislike the way the word 'engagement' is used. Too often talked about as a biennial measure, rather than the everyday action of connecting with the people around us.

But the good news? According to a Towers Watson study, companies that communicate effectively are four times more likely to have higher engagement levels, and have 47 per cent higher shareholder returns compared with less proficient businesses. Not to mention a whole bag of other benefits to communicating better.

**If we were to write a song about business based on daily conversations with leaders, we'd call it 'Seeking Engagement'.**

## Call the spade a bloody shovel

Just as we were finishing this book, one of Australia's largest banks, National Australia Bank (NAB), farewelled 6000 employees. To put that number in perspective, that's one in every five people in their workforce. It wasn't because of a downturn either — quite the opposite. The news came the same day the bank announced a profit of over five billion clams (which is a whole lot of chowder by anyone's reckoning).

Artificial intelligence is already changing our business landscape. In the case of NAB, automation was inevitable. They weren't the first and they certainly won't be the last organisation whose workforce experiences changes to the number and types of roles available, and the skills required for the times ahead.

The teams we'll lead in the very near future (if we aren't already) will be vastly different. As leaders, the ability to go beyond our technical expertise and embrace our human skills will be what keeps us relevant: inspiring people to do their best work; helping them navigate change; promoting problem solving and innovation; keeping them safe, healthy and happy. Making a difference. Creating a legacy. These are the hallmarks of a leader skilled in the art of influence.

*Influence.* Such a wonderful word, don't you think? Influence is subtle, encouraging. Influence suggests a light touch, a gentle hand. Influence is a leadership skill that is infinitely preferable to its jerk cousin, *manipulation.*

Influence promotes change for the benefit of all involved. Unlike manipulation, which is purely in our own interests (or sick pleasure, for those of a sadistic bent). But let's just call a spade a shovel and say it simply: 'Influence and manipulation are both about making people do what we bloody well want them to do!' With influence, though, there's a caveat: ' … so everyone wins'.

So what does it take to become an influential leader?

Choose any heavyweight through history, and consider what you remember about them. Perhaps it's Winston Churchill rallying England through war, or Martin Luther King Jr taking a stand for civil rights, or Steve Jobs making Apple relevant again.

Thinking about these individuals, we tend to remember their words and the way they used them. Their ability to tell stories and evoke emotion. The way they could persuade and move people through powerful speeches and conversations.

*'We shall fight on the beaches … '*

*'I have a dream … '*

*'Here's to the crazy ones … '*

Yes, their ability to influence came from exceptional communication skills. Using language to inspire people and bring them together; using words, imagery and narratives to evoke emotions; using conversations to share the knowledge that shapes a better tomorrow. Without influence, nothing changes; no-one changes.

## Human versus goldfish

Life is busy and work is busier. We live in a connected world, constantly beset by a barrage of priorities competing for our eyes, ears and minds.

Every day we're bombarded with emails, meetings, memos, posters, phone calls, messages and all kinds of asynchronous communications: Yammer, Slack, various message platforms—and the socials. Our days are crammed with more and more. Our attention spans, stretched to breaking.

What were we talking about again? Oho! Cute, but seriously... will you look at that bird. You get the point, or perhaps we've rambled too long and you've drifted onto Instagram or email... or whatever else blows wind into your spinnaker.

To survive amidst the noise and clutter, we've become skilled at sifting irrelevant or unexciting information. This makes attention a valuable resource—a finite one at that. And, like any other business resource, be it money, machinery, time or space, attention should be wisely invested in, carefully managed and never, ever squandered.

**To survive amidst the noise and clutter, we've become skilled at sifting irrelevant or unexciting information.**

Yes, attention is more difficult to capture than ever before, and we're well past being able to rely on expectation. Expecting people to read a manual, to learn a new process, to know a policy, to give us their full and undivided attention. Our people are far too busy simply trying to do their jobs for us to expect expectation to work.

If we want people's attention, we need to get smarter. Or risk wasting a ton of time and money developing well-intentioned, potentially brilliant strategies, programs and initiatives that fail before they get off the ground. Not because they weren't good, and not because they weren't necessary, but simply because no-one paid them any attention.

So how do we earn attention?

Well, to begin with, we need to WAKE THEM UP! We need to draw people in, make them curious, make them laugh, surprise them, tantalise them with stories, appeal to their eyeballs, be relevant and interesting—and, for the love of furry kittens, make them *feel* something. *Anything.*

In many cases, it won't be easy. The greater the noise, the greater the filter—the more we need to tune our signal.

# How to speak whaaat?

In the pages ahead you'll find 11 strategies we use every day to help leaders seize attention, win hearts and move minds. These strategies can be used in any context, no matter your role, industry or organisation size. While we frequently refer to 'leaders', this isn't bound by job title. To us, a leader is anyone with the gumption to bring about change for the benefit of everyone.

Each strategy contains theories, science and practical ideas, illustrated by examples of leaders who've used the strategy effectively. These stories are real — actual projects we've been thrilled to work on with some truly amazing folk. All that's been changed is their name and the company they work for (because: legal departments). While these stories are used in isolation to illustrate the strategies, they're typically part of a much larger plan.

Finally, it's not all kittens and sunbeams. There are three areas for wariness. These 'bewares' detail the biggest challenges we face on our pursuit of speaking human. Understanding and overcoming these potential perils is essential to producing work that gains attention, engages and influences.

You can read this book chronologically from cover to cover, or skip gleefully through it in any order you please. There's no right or wrong way to attack it. Except backwards. That would be plain perverse (unless of course you're reading this in Hebrew, Arabic or tategaki) ... but we digress.

Ready?

Onwards...

# Curiosity

## The insatiable hunger of a curious mind

Was it the cover of this book that seduced you? The witty title, unexpected and exuding a certain look-twice irony? A smirk amidst shelves stuffed with serious business.

Yes, indeed! It was *curiosity* that drew your attention and compelled you to drag this book from the shelf. The irrepressible desire to acquire new knowledge or learn new skills.

Curiosity, the drive to explore, investigate, innovate, helped our species develop and evolve—pushed us to greatness. Driven by curiosity, we climbed the highest peaks and dived to the deepest depths. We braved world-edges and sea monsters to sail around the world, discovering new continents filled with exotic oddities.

Curiosity prompted us to dress in bulky white suits and strap ourselves into too-thin tin space shuttles stuffed with enough explosives to quite literally blow ourselves to the moon. Curiosity helped us make fire, then electricity. Curiosity gave us bacon on pancakes, all smothered in maple syrup. Perhaps not always in our best interests, but the outcomes were almost always interesting.

More importantly, it's every bit as relevant and influential at work. Curiosity draws our attention and primes us to learn. It has the power to shift mindsets. It can even change the relationships we have with others.

Picture the typical organisation-led leadership program. Someone spots a capability gap in their mid-tier managers. The need for an organisation-wide leadership program is proclaimed, and the usual flurry of activity ensues. Heads nod, learning objectives are identified, speakers are booked, working sessions are arranged, and six months later the program is good to go.

Once backs have been slapped for a job well done, an email is sent to all mid-tier managers requesting their attendance on a particular date. On an inspiration scale from one to William Wallace bellowing 'FREEDOM!', the email hits around a one point five. Thirty per cent miss the email altogether. Ten per cent saw it but thought it was spam and didn't apply to them. Twenty per cent get their backs up because they don't need a bloody leadership program. The rest are quietly disgruntled at the prospect of taking time out of their busy schedules.

Friends, there's another way—a better way. And it begins with *curiosity*.

## Curiosity draws our attention

Life is full of countless curiosities vying for our interest. Yet the systemised and routine nature of many roles means people are exposed to far fewer sources of curiosity at work. This gives us the ideal opportunity to use curiosity to draw attention to an upcoming program, event or initiative.

## Curiosity is a primer for learning

When something intrigues us, we're compelled to investigate. And when we're inquisitive enough, it completely consumes us. This makes curiosity ridiculously effective at priming people to learn. By getting folk curious before dropping knowledge, we put them in the ideal state for experimenting, discovering, learning and improving.

## Curiosity improves our relationships

Being naturally curious about something is completely different from being *told* to be interested in it. There's a subtle yet powerful shift in mindset that happens when we choose to opt in. We're more focused, committed to learning and actively engaged.

This is because when we encourage curiosity, it extends an invitation rather than issuing a command. It pushes us out of a parent–child or sergeant–soldier model, into a better type of relationship. It puts the onus on the individual to learn, promoting accountability and autonomy. It allows adults to be, well, adults—taking responsibility for their own personal development rather than expecting everything to be delivered on the proverbial silver platter.

## You won't believe what happens next...

In the early nineties, a fellow named George Loewenstein identified the psychological phenomenon whereby we're at our most curious when there's a gap between what we know and what we want to know. An almost obsessive need to close this gap triggers an emotional response—much like a cognitive itch that we desperately want to scratch and only relieve by filling in the blanks.

Loewenstein's theory found that we can intentionally provoke curiosity by providing a small amount of information while withholding the rest.

A Caltech study discovered a direct correlation between how much we know and how curious we are to learn more. Researchers took 40 students, an fMRI machine and a quiz...and what happened next isn't the punchline to a nerdy scientist joke. No, they didn't walk into a bar, but they did find out that we're most curious when we know only a little about a subject, up until we have a moderate amount of knowledge, at which point our curiosity steadily decreases. This means that curiosity is often contextual, based on each person's unique knowledge and experience.

Marketing and advertising copywriters have been exploiting the curiosity gap to gain our attention and influence our behaviour for years. Clickbait headlines tease us with just enough information to pique our curiosity, promising a satisfying revelation with just one click.

*He was reunited with his cat after several years of separation. What happens next will leave you speechless...*

Despite knowing exactly what those devious marketing devils are doing, damned if I don't pound that link with grudging enthusiasm to find out the ending of this heart-warming tale of man and beast.

Speaking of small furry critters, lean in close, and let your old pals tell you a tale about Kerrie and her rabbits.

## Kerrie and the rabbits

Growth is tough, and this rapidly scaling fintech start-up experienced the typical pains. How to keep the close-knit culture they'd enjoyed as a small team as they headed towards becoming a company where it was difficult to remember everyone's name?

Kerrie, Head of People, Leadership and Culture, recognised that to keep their culture strong, they needed to establish a rhythm of communication that would provide ongoing triggers for their vision, values and mission. Bringing rigour to the growing company was necessary, but just as important was staying true to their fun and youthful culture. In short, they wanted to grow up but not grow old.

Kerrie's communication strategy began with a simple idea. She wanted to launch the strategy in a way that captured the attention of the young, savvy and busy crew, and she wanted to shine a spotlight on the company's mission 'to delight'. But how to do it in a way that would break people out of their typical patterns and routines and snare their attention?

The solution? A simple concept that captured curiosity and inspired delight.

Each morning, employees entered the foyer bleary-eyed to discover a new poster featuring a famous bunny from popular culture (the company's logo is a rabbit). From the Easter Bunny to the Playboy Bunny, this was the full gamut of rabbit. The posters were minimal: just a stylised rabbit's head and a word that corresponded to the value it was known for. Like, the Energizer Bunny and stamina, Bugs Bunny and mischief, the Playboy Bunny and ... happy endings.

Every day, employees paused to identify the recently added rabbit, and conversations would begin. 'Why are they here?' and 'What are they for?' Followed by, 'Do you remember the first time you watched *Donnie Darko*?' and, 'Mmm … Jake Gyllenhaal.'

To keep these conversations going, for the duration of the campaign Kerrie ran a competition to identify each of the bunnies. This had people Googling famous rabbits, comparing prospective answers with the words on the poster. At the end of the competition, winners were promised a framed rabbit poster of their choice.

On the nineteenth day, the final poster was hung. It showed the company's logo with the word 'delight' underneath. An all-in meeting had been organised for that afternoon, and while the rabbits were still fresh in everyone's mind, Kerrie introduced the communication strategy. She outlined what it was about and what it meant for everyone. More importantly, she explained how getting more rigorous around communication didn't mean selling out or becoming dull and corporate; it meant doing it in a way that stayed true to always delivering delight.

## We can't help ourselves

What made Kerrie's campaign so successful? The investment was small, the implementation easy. Yet each morning most employees would pause, look up from their phones, take the time to examine the posters and even instigate conversations about rabbits.

The campaign captured people's attention for the same reason all unsolved mysteries fascinate and captivate us. What happened to the *Mary Celeste*? Who was Jack the Ripper, really? What strangeness transpires in the Bermuda Triangle? Is there really a Loch Ness monster? Is there other intelligent life out there in the universe, and if so, is it really intent on probing us inappropriately?

The curiosity gap does more than attract our attention; it compels us to learn.

Evan Polman and researchers at the University of Wisconsin–Madison conducted several experiments to find out how effective the curiosity gap was in influencing people's decision making and behaviours. Their study offered 200 participants a choice between a plain cookie and a delicious, chocolate-dipped, sprinkle-burnished biscuit. Which did most choose? The answer is obvious. Or is it?

In a cruel twist, the researchers told half the participants that the plain biscuit was a fortune cookie with a personalised message inside. In the group who weren't given this additional information, a very sensible 80 per cent chose the superior chocolate-dipped cookie. But out of the group who were told the plain biscuit was a fortune cookie, 71 per cent chose the plain biscuit. Curiosity alone caused a majority to make an undeniably inferior cookie choice.

**The curiosity gap does more than attract our attention; it compels us to learn.** Other studies confirm that we'll go to more effort simply to satisfy our curiosity. Polman and pals increased the use of stairs in a university building by roughly 10 per cent just by posting trivia questions near the elevator and promising that answers could be found in the stairwell.

Enabling behaviour change is one of the biggest challenges facing any leader. Yet it turns out there's no need for sticks or carrots. Curiosity alone is enough to motivate people to change their own behaviours, even if it means investing more effort or choosing a less desirable outcome.

These findings demonstrate how effective curiosity can be as a catalyst or trigger to gain attention and begin the process of forming new habits. The next challenge is ensuring change is embedded.

### Yuvan attempts to lick his elbow

Workplace health and wellness campaigns can easily fall into the eye-rollingly obvious territory of 'eat healthier food' and 'exercise more'. They're even more challenging when you work for one of the largest producers of soft drinks and snack foods. Yuvan, a mid-level manager tasked with the job of rolling out a better health campaign, knew he'd have to bring a fresh approach to a tired topic if he was going to cut through and make a difference.

Yuvan chose to focus on the less frequently discussed areas of health and wellness, like sleeping better, moving better, thinking better and connecting better. The roll-out was comprehensive, including conversation kits for managers, along with digital and environmental triggers. However, it was the content that caught people's attention.

Rather than taking the typical approach, Yuvan led with curiosity. For 'Connect Better', the headline of the poster read: 'DID YOU KNOW THAT IT'S IMPOSSIBLE TO LICK YOUR OWN ELBOW?' paired with a stylised image of someone attempting the feat.

Inevitably people tried. You can't throw down a gauntlet like that and not have people thrusting tongue vainly at funny bone (admit it, you're resisting the urge to give it a go right now!). And inevitably the resulting contortions attracted the attention of passers-by, who stopped to quiz the aspiring elbow-lickers as to what on earth they were doing.

Much hilarity ensued, with energetic efforts to help one another reach the unreachable, and conversations around who knew about this elbow caper. The follow-up material identified how all these things—laughter, touch and conversations—increase trust and foster better relationships. The result? Not only did everyone *understand* the concept of connecting better, but they were actually *engaged* in connecting better.

Each focus area used a similar approach: a 'Did you know…' fact that made people curious to find out more. The initiative was so successful that although it started in Australia, it soon spread around the world.

## We were born curious

Perhaps the best news is that curiosity isn't something we need to learn. We're curious from the moment we're pushed out into this world, and it plays a major role in our development from infancy through childhood.

It makes sense that to survive and evolve our species would be wired to be curious. Are those red berries edible? Masticate and hope for the best. If we live to tell the tale, it's good news for us, but even better news for the tribe, who now have a whole new food source.

Behind our curious behaviour is an active mind and pleasurable chemicals. fMRI scans of an inquisitive brain reveal a notable increase in activity in three areas: the left caudate, the prefrontal cortex and the parahippocampal gyrus.

The caudate is of particular interest (perhaps because no-one can pronounce or remember the name of the gyrating hippopotamus region). Linked to learning, the caudate's a real giver, a pleasure centre responsible for all sorts of wonderful feelings when stimulated with new information. Our desire for knowledge begins as a dopamine craving in the same primal pathway that responds to sex, drugs, and rock and roll. 🤘

Yes, we're all junkies, of sorts. Brain engorged with new knowledge, you're probably high right now. Do you feel it? Dopamine, serotonin and opioids—all rushing through your brain, rewarding you for your curiosity.

Don't fight it. Just relax…

## Mya and the Blarney Stone (Part I)

Every year, Mya's team come together from around the world for their annual summit. It's a chance to meet other team members who have previously existed only as disembodied voices in phone calls, or sporadic email conversations.

This year, Mya, Director of Digitalisation and Governance, decided the summit would be different. It wasn't that previous years had been mediocre, but the theme for the upcoming year, *Better Bolder Clearer Stronger*, meant lifting the experience to match her lofty ideal.

Mya wanted people to enter the event with a different mindset. But instead of just telling people the event would be different from previous years, she decided to *demonstrate* that it would be better, bolder, clearer and, yes, stronger too.

Her first point of contact with attendees was exactly the opposite of the explicit, detail-heavy email invitation often used for work functions. Instead, over a five-week period leading up to the summit, she delivered a weekly hand-drawn video sharing facts about the venue (Cork, Ireland), tied loosely to one of the four themes.

In the first video, attendees learned about Cork's traditions of standing strong in the face of adversity dating all the way back to the Viking raids of the ninth century (Better Together). The second video shared the story of Sir Walter Raleigh coaxing the first potato from the rich soils around Cork (Bolder Aspirations). The third video revealed the legend of the Blarney Stone, and how kissing it would grant the gift of the gab (Clearer Communication). The fourth video informed attendees that Cork is home to the largest pot still in the world (Stronger Performance). Only in the fifth and final video, five weeks later, were attendees given a more traditional invitation to the event, along with an explanation of the four themes.

The videos were short, no more than 40 seconds each, with simple images hand-drawn onto one page over the duration of the clip. And the response was terrific. Mya received great feedback on the videos, but, more importantly, everyone said how much they were looking forward to experiencing something different.

## We remember the peripherals

The summit was an event attendees already looked forward to, but Mya and her team's teaser videos amplified their excitement by focusing on the unfamiliar destination.

Studies have found that curiosity not only primes us to learn about a specific topic, but also helps us remember peripheral and incidental information around the topic.

Neuroscientist Charan Ranganath rounded up 19 people and showed them a list containing over 100 questions. Participants rated each question on how curious they were to know the answer, then fMRI was used to monitor their brain activity while they reviewed their highest-rated questions. After looking at each question for 14 seconds, they were shown a photo of a completely unrelated person, then given the answer.

Later, participants were tested to see how well they recalled both the answers and faces. In a fascinating revelation, Ranganath found that the more curious people were about a question, the more likely they were to remember not only the answer, but also the face that preceded it. A follow-up test a day later confirmed the results. Curiosity primes learning and memory, but it isn't just confined to the specific content we're studying; it includes any peripheral information we're exposed to at the same time.

Mya's campaign worked perfectly by focusing on the part of the experience that attendees had only a small amount of knowledge about: the destination. This prompted curiosity that bled into interest in the summit itself. And rather than telling people that the event would be different, she allowed attendees to form the impression themselves, based on the format and content of the messaging.

## Stone-cold killers of curiosity

So — there must be a catch, right?

Well, yes. Curiosity can captivate us so completely that there's the risk of enjoying the journey more than the destination. And while we definitely want people to thrill to the process of discovery, we also want to ensure their expectations are met so they finish on a high.

When it comes to avoiding a tepid conclusion, we need to consider three stone-cold killers of curiosity.

### Unrealistic expectations

If we want people to be satisfied with the results of their curious endeavours, we need to manage their expectations early. Promising specific outcomes can be risky, as it can set potentially unrealistic beliefs. It's far better to promise (and deliver) an enjoyable discovery experience.

## A good time, not a long time

Time is also an important factor in maintaining curiosity. Studies show that when we don't expect to resolve our curiosity in a reasonable time, we're more likely to get frustrated and lose interest.

Questions left hanging too long, or information shared too slowly or sporadically, can throw a big wet blanket over curiosity, which is obviously exactly the opposite of what we want to achieve. In most cases, we can avert potential problems through proper planning. However, in situations where long timeframes are unavoidable, we should consider making progress visible to maintain motivation.

## Fear of failure

Of all the threats to curiosity, fear is the quickest killer of motivation. This is the perception (correct or not) that we might not be capable of satisfying our interest.

This is a crucial consideration when designing learning or development programs. We need to ensure learning is achievable, even if it means catering to different ability levels rather than taking a one-size-fits-all approach. More importantly, we need to ensure people believe they're capable of success.

We also need to be wary of discouraging curious behaviours. As many organisations place increasing importance on innovation, curiosity is a valuable quality to find and foster in people. However, with innovation comes risk and uncertainty.

**Punishing failure is a great way to crush future curiosity—and potential brilliance along with it.**

The truth is that curiosity doesn't always lead to organisation-changing ideas and industry-changing innovation. It can just as easily lead to a magnificent failure. And there's the rub. Punishing failure is a great way to crush future curiosity—and potential brilliance along with it.

# How to speak...
# curiosity

### Idea #01: Make it incomplete

Make it... incomplete? Sounds counterintuitive, doesn't it? But, as Loewenstein, Kerrie, Yuvan and Mya all realised, we're most curious when we have a small amount of information and the rest is withheld.* Our need to close the curiosity gap — the gap between what we know and what we want to know — drives us crazy.

To make our communication incomplete, we can:

- Tease people with a small amount of information while withholding the rest.

- Drip-feed content in small amounts to keep people hungry for more.

- Provide information as a puzzle or quiz for people to fill in the blanks.

- Consider segmenting communication where significant differences in knowledge or experience exist. The curiosity gap is more effective when we know a small to moderate amount.

---

* This is a tactic best left for positive things — never bad news. No-one wants to be drip-fed hints about their impending sacking.

## Idea #02: Make it intriguing

We're fascinated by mysteries and puzzles. They capture our imagination and inspire us to wonder at the possibilities. In our tale about Kerrie and her rabbits, the appearance of a new poster each day was a mystery that prompted speculation. What were they about? How long would it go on for? When would we find out the purpose?

How can we incorporate more mystery into our communication? We're glad you asked!

To make our communication intriguing, we can:

- Use teaser campaigns in the lead-up to programs, events or initiatives, rather than jumping straight to making explicit announcements.

- Lead with questions rather than statements — they inspire curiosity and open a conversation.

- Use quizzes for learning — they invite a more active approach.

- Allow people the opportunity to sate their curiosity in a reasonable time.

## Idea #03: Make it novel

We're curious about anything unfamiliar, shiny or new. The lead-up to Mya's summit used an offbeat approach to pre-event communication. It was unorthodox in every aspect, from the medium to the message to the illustration style.

To bring novelty into our communication, we can:

- Look at what we've done in the past, especially the things we do frequently — then do them differently.

- Bring something entirely new to our communication. This might be a new channel or medium, or an entirely new style.

- Look beyond our own preferences, interests and experience, and consider what others might find unique.

- Find out what's being done in other industries, and adapt those ideas to our contexts.

## Idea #04: Make it unpredictable

We're lulled by routine and repetition; anything that falls outside the usual context captures our curiosity. This isn't to say that routine is bad or that we need to take a wrecking ball to *everything*. But if we want attention, we need to shake things up.*

To make our communication unpredictable, we can:

- Build a rhythm of unpredictability and delight. Consistency, consistency, consistency—grenade! Enough consistency to feel comfortable … then hit them with something new to grab their attention.

- Change things up regularly to avoid complacency. Create structures with the flexibility to evolve. Switch up traditions and regular events to keep them interesting.

- Find peripheral information that's in some way related to the subject, rather than leading with obvious headlines. One or two steps sideways from the primary content is where we find some of the most interesting and attention-grabbing material.

* Another area for caution, friends. Times of organisational unrest aren't the best time for lobbing communication hand grenades, no matter how delightful.

# Anticipation

## The exquisite agony
## of anticipation

That feeling of waiting for a parcel to navigate the postal system to arrive in our mailbox; booking a holiday, then the impatience and excitement as the departure date too slowly approaches; watching a trailer for a new movie, then the months dragging by before it appears on screen ...

That heady blend of impatience, expectation and excitement is *anticipation*.

Anticipation segues very satisfactorily from curiosity, because it's the transition from *wondering* to *predicting*, *guessing* and *hoping*. It relies on our having just enough information to form vague expectations, yet retains enough ambiguity to offer the potential for surprise and delight.

While we need to take an active approach to satisfying our curiosity, anticipation is a more passive state. It's the way we *feel* while waiting for something to happen. But although it exists without external influence, when we manage people's anticipation we can hold their attention more effectively, get them into the right mindset, and ensure their expectations are met or exceeded.

While we were furiously pounding away at the final paragraphs of this book, the 2018 Commonwealth Games were happening right outside our office. This may conjure a mental image of packs of athletes in too-tight spandex sweating their way along palm-lined roads with banner-waving crowds cheering them on, but many areas of the Gold Coast were curiously quiet. We noticed that many of our neighbours had fled town, but why leave during the biggest event in years?

Rewind six months to the lead-up to this historic event. Anticipation was high, and expectations were mixed. Residents were unsure how the event would impact them. Would there be more traffic? Road closures? Would it even be possible to get to work?

The City of Gold Coast went to great lengths to help residents 'Get Set For The Games'. Letterbox drops with detailed information on road closures, alternative suggestions for getting to work, parking and public transport options, and numerous ways to deal with the impending mayhem. It was a thoroughly commendable job at ensuring logistical tranquillity by the time the Games rolled around. And it worked, entirely too well.

The campaign confirmed everyone's worst fears — it was going to be UTTER CHAOS! Any excitement about the event was quickly overwhelmed by the potential inconvenience. And although some residents stayed and enjoyed the Games, just as many let their homes as holiday rentals and left the Coast. As a result, many of the city's most vibrant suburbs lay eerily deserted, the occasional helicopter beating overhead adding to a decidedly post-apocalyptic vibe. Ahh … we do exaggerate ever so slightly for effect.

It's a perfect example of how managing (or mismanaging) expectations effectively can make a massive difference, and it's every bit as critical to consider at work.

### Anticipation is a natural period of attention

Anticipation inevitably follows the announcement or launch of any initiative, event or program. This is the time we have people's attention, but it isn't the moment to sit back and expect them to remain interested. It's an opportunity to strategically map out touchpoints that keep people focused and engaged over the duration.

### Anticipation is an opportunity to influence mindset

We can also use the state of anticipation to shape or influence how people feel. If there's an expectation that safety conferences are always boring, we can use messaging during the anticipation period to flip those beliefs. We just need to be mindful of the expectations we're amplifying. In the case of the Commonwealth Games, the 'Get Set' campaign reinforced residents' assumptions that the Games were going to cause disruption. The messaging was full of important information, but perhaps it would've been better to foster a little excitement first.

## Anticipation is the time to manage expectations

Work is a series of expectations. We have beliefs around what we (and others) should or shouldn't be paid; the hours we should or shouldn't be working; the decisions our leaders should or shouldn't be making; the directions our company should or shouldn't be taking; and who should or shouldn't be employed, let alone promoted. Over time, all these unmet expectations compound and slowly erode engagement.

Using anticipation to manage others' expectations leads to stronger connections with our work, and with each other. Very conveniently (and certainly not accidentally), this is the perfect time to revisit Mya and her team, and discover how they managed attendees' anticipation by directing it towards the various aspects of the coming experience.

## Mya and the Blarney Stone (Part II)

Over the five-week lead-up period, summit attendees moved through states of curiosity, anticipation and expectation.

After receiving the first video, people were curious. What was this all about? It was a very different start from previous summits, and it captured their attention. Many hadn't visited Ireland before, and the videos piqued their interest.

Attendees were quickly sucked back into the preoccupations of work, but after the second, third and fourth videos their anticipation spiked. After the second video, anticipation also shifted from

(continued)

## Mya and the Blarney Stone (Part II) (continued)

the summit to include the communication medium. The regular delivery meant that people began to expect and look forward to the next video.

The fifth video finally revealed the details, showing how the summit would be different from previous years in format, content, style and networking opportunities.

Ah yes, *networking*... a word that has the power to divide any group. A word with a sound that rings ever so sweetly to extroverts, while driving most introverts into nervous sweats. But despite the potential for untold awkwardness and social indignities ranging from poorly executed handshakes to name amnesia, networking is an essential part of business events. For medium-sized businesses, it's a chance to strengthen relationships. For global organisations, it's an opportunity to meet and connect with colleagues from around the world.

Harper, Global Operations Training and Communication Specialist, was responsible for the social side of the summit. She recognised that networking can be a minefield if not facilitated properly. To ensure the event met expectations, Harper collected details from every attendee (including their birthplace, superpower of choice, one thing they could eat/drink forever and something no-one would guess about them) and integrated them, along with a stylised headshot, into the local currency to produce 'networking money'.

On arrival at the summit, attendees were given a wad of bills that they could distribute as icebreakers. And distribute them they did—with gleeful abandon. So much so that it was difficult to draw them out of conversation and money exchange, and into scheduled activity.

## The thrill of the chase

Like curiosity, anticipation is hardwired into us. We're no better than animals with a thrill for the chase—dopamine lathering us up in jittery anticipation, heightening our emotions. It's a good thing too, because without this inherent enthusiasm for the hunt or harvest, we might have starved ourselves into extinction a long time ago.

Anticipation is rooted in the cerebellum, a primal part of the brain that controls our automatic behaviours. But it's the chemicals that make anticipation such a potent emotion. While dopamine has traditionally been thought of as a pleasure chemical, recent research by neuroscientist Robert Sapolsky suggests it's actually an *anticipation* of pleasure chemical. Yes, we get our real kicks from anticipating the reward, rather than receiving it.

Another similarity to curiosity is the potential for the period of anticipation to be more enjoyable than the subsequent experience. This is due to our tendency to feel more strongly about the future than the present or past.

Researchers in the Netherlands studied the relationship between travel and happiness in a group of 1530 people. They discovered that while a holiday (predictably) made people happier, the real peak in pleasure came before they even left home. The anticipation of travel was a more powerful driver of happiness than the holiday itself, or their memories of it afterwards.

Similarly, Marketing professor Marsha Richins discovered that even the most materialistic consumers derive more pleasure from the anticipation of a purchase than from the purchase itself. Simply thinking about buying something, regardless of size or expense, elicited strong, positive emotions including joy, excitement and optimism. Even more fascinating, however, was the correlation between the strength of people's emotions during anticipation and their expectations. The more a person thought the purchase would change their lives, the stronger their anticipation, but also the greater their disappointment if their expectations weren't met.

## Managing expectations

So how do anticipation and expectations interact?

Well, at the most basic level, anticipation can be positive or negative. The way we feel is usually determined by our expectations—our beliefs, predictions or hopes that a specific outcome will occur. If we expect something bad to happen, we experience emotions like anxiety or fear. When we think something good is likely to occur (which fortunately we're biased towards), we feel pleasure, hope or excitement.

Our expectations are usually contextual, based on personal beliefs, existing information and memories of past experiences. However, they can also be influenced by external sources. Advertising and marketing rely on expectation to make us buy things we don't really need—overpromising and overselling the benefits a product or service will have on our lives.

> It may look like an ordinary kitchen knife, but this space-grade magnesium marvel will cut through three slabs of granite and still slice you up a mean chow mein...

This approach can be just as common inside organisations. Overhyping the really quite mundane, launching programs that are unworthy of launch. It's natural to get excited about a new initiative, and it's perfectly normal we'd want to share our work. Yet no matter how well intentioned, overexuberance leads to disappointment if others' expectations aren't met.

**Of all the possible outcomes for anticipation and expectation, the least desirable scenario is _confusion_.** Worse, with each failure to deliver, we make it tougher to get everyone excited again when we have something truly worthy of their enthusiasm.

Yes, with expectation comes the potential for disappointment.

So let's ease that burden. We don't need to be blowing people out of the water on every occasion. In many situations, simply delivering the expected is actually a very good thing. Yale University professor of Psychiatry, Neurobiology and Pharmacology Marina Picciotto proposes that happiness occurs only when our circumstances _match_ our expectations.

Of all the possible outcomes for anticipation and expectation, the least desirable scenario is _confusion_. Confusion occurs when we have very specific expectations based on past experiences, but the reality differs dramatically.

# How to speak…
# anticipation

### Idea #05: Control the pace

Timing is critical when it comes to managing anticipation. We need to consider when it starts, how long it lasts and how often we experience it. All these factors make a big difference.

We also need to consider whether the anticipation is positive or negative. When we're really looking forward to something, we're prone to impatience. And when we're dreading something, anticipation can cause anxiety. These are both times to avoid dragging out anticipation.

To control the pace, we can:

- Ensure people know about the truly transformative ideas, initiatives, events and programs before they happen. Last-minute announcements rob people of the opportunity for anticipation, removing an important part of the experience.

- Match the duration of anticipation with the importance of the experience. Modest experiences warrant only short periods of anticipation, while big or important events deserve more time.

- Limit the time spent anticipating bad news or an unpleasant event. No-one wants to drag out the experience of an axe coming down. Bad news is best delivered fast.

- Limit the time spent anticipating something really exciting. There's only so long we can stay enthusiastic before the feeling shifts to impatience.

- Create a series of smaller experiences and interactions to foster ongoing anticipation, instead of directing all our attention to one large outcome. Frequency beats intensity; looking forward to several small experiences makes us happier than anticipating one big event.

## Idea #06: Manage expectations

Let's use the anticipation period to manage expectations, build excitement (when appropriate) and use cognitive framing to influence the experience ahead. Remember, we don't need people to be overenthusiastically anticipating absolutely everything. In many cases, effectively managing anticipation means simply *meeting* people's expectations.

To manage expectations, we can:

- Avoid big announcements when an occasion doesn't warrant anticipation.

- Use anti-hype when expectations are higher than we can deliver on, and there's a risk of disappointment. This is also an effective tactic for a group that's cynical or sceptical, or in situations that don't warrant unnecessary fanfare. To play it down, we can drop some reality and focus on the challenges, as long as we don't swing the pendulum too far the other way and leave people with negative expectations.

- Encourage anticipation without specific expectations. Keep people in the moment — mindful and open-minded, wondering at the possibilities and anticipating challenges. This is known as *anticipatory thinking*. It's not about crystal balls, tarot cards or guessing the future. It's about trying to prepare and adapt for whatever possibility the future throws our way.

- Amplify expectations, but only when we're confident we can exceed them. The most memorable experiences occur when we're excited yet the outcome exceeds our expectations.

# Surprise!
## The unanticipated delight
## of the unexpected

———

When a title is 'Surprise!', one tends to feel a burden of responsibility—an obligation, really—to make at least a half-hearted effort to demonstrate the point. Something unexpected. Something unique. Something that breaks the structure, bursts from the page and wrenches your wandering eyes and minds right back to giving us your undivided attention.

Surely, though, such trickery and gimmicks would've been (at least subconsciously) expected, and therefore not very surprising at all. An insult to your intelligence, even. So we settled for what we hope you'll find a slightly ironic, yet understatedly poignant exclamation mark.

Surprise! ☺

In a time when we Google away the unexpected by thoroughly investigating every potential purchase or experience, surprises are becoming far too infrequent. Which is unfortunate, really. Because surprise captures our attention, piques our curiosity, motivates us to learn, keeps us engaged and creates memories that are more easily recalled.

When designing employee experiences, we often use a driving emotions activity to help project leads identify how they want people to feel as the experience unfolds. One of the emotions we often discuss is surprise. And, it's no surprise that when working with safety leaders in particular, this suggestion is almost always met with a resounding, 'Hells no!', followed by, 'we can't surprise people when we're talking about risk'. We get it, no-one wants a surprise safety incident at work. But when we're talking about how people feel while they're experiencing safety, or any other initiative for that matter, perhaps we shouldn't write off surprise so quickly.

When we want to seize people's attention quickly, reframe the typically dull or predicable, or keep people engaged over the long term—surprise gets it done.

## Surprise jolts us back to attention

Days, weeks, months, years and careers all roll together; we're lulled by repetition and routine. Systems and processes put us into efficiency autopilot. Which makes sense, right? Good for productivity, great for the profits! But it also makes snapping people out of a work-induced coma, and back to attention, challenging. When we need to be brought to attention quickly, when we need laser focus—surprise shakes us alert.

## Surprise breaks our expectations

Surprises don't all need to be earth-shattering revelations. Some of the best surprises happen when we go beyond people's expectations when they least expect it. Perhaps it's redesigning a typically dull, technical handbook to make it more appealing. This seemingly trivial change can be enough to reframe the way people engage with the content, increasing the likelihood of making a difference.

## Surprise stimulates long-term engagement

One of the toughest parts of keeping folk engaged is dealing with the inevitability that their interest will wane over time. Surprise is the ultimate breaker of apathy. By using it discerningly at key moments, we can switch things up to bring people's attention to important areas — company vision, values, sales, safety or whatever it is for you.

## Mashing the pause button

To drop some science, surprise is a brief physiological, psychological and emotional state. It's a startle response experienced by humans (and animals) as the result of an unexpected event.

To turn that human, it's the equivalent of mashing a pause button in our brain. When we experience something new or unexpected, surprise makes us stop what we're doing, hijacks our attention, redirects our focus and forces us to pay attention to a new, possibly important event.

This process relies on our hippocampus declaring the stimulus surprising. This is the area of our brain responsible for identifying, processing and storing new sensory impressions. Think of the hippocampus as a gatekeeper — a novelty detector for incoming information. When it identifies new or unfamiliar information, it responds with a gleeful ejaculation of dopamine that does a victory lap around the brain before coming right back to the hippocampus. This is known as the hippocampal-SN/VTA loop, a decidedly scientific-sounding process responsible for forming long-term memories.

Although we've just spent several paragraphs labouring through the way it works, our response happens extremely quickly — done and dusted in a mere 3–8 milliseconds.

Once again, like curiosity and anticipation, surprise makes sense from a survival perspective. Imagine: you're swaddled in furs and walking through an ancient forest when a giant lizard bursts from the undergrowth with ill intentions in its reptilian eyes. *Surprise!* The startle reflex just saved your life.

We're no longer facing life and death situations every day, but our response to surprise remains undiminished. And provides us with a very handy little tactic we can use to seize people's attention.

## Mya and the Blarney Stone (Part III)

Let's return one last time to our story about Mya and her annual summit. But let's look at the lead-up to the summit from a slightly different perspective.

When the first video arrived unexpectedly in the attendees' inboxes, all hand-drawn whimsy and narrated in a thick Irish brogue, speaking of rebellion and Viking raiders, the obvious reaction was surprise. Everything about the communication was different from the typical event invitation. The medium, the style, the content—all defied previous experience and expectations.

The second video also came as a surprise, but by the third and fourth week attendees were ready and had shifted to a state of anticipation.

## A catalyst for change

You might be thinking we've already attributed the success of Mya's campaign to curiosity *and* anticipation. Are we now claiming that surprise also played a role?

Indeed we did, and we certainly are.

It's not laziness that led us to recycle the same story for curiosity, anticipation and surprise—there's a close relationship between the three. When something is familiar, anticipated or expected, we know how to respond: nothing to see here, folks. But if it's new or unexpected, we're surprised, and that makes us curious to find out more.

While theories of motivation and learning go in and out of fashion, it's been widely accepted since the mid 20th century that unexpected events are one of the primary drivers of seeking new knowledge.

A Johns Hopkins study discovered that surprise is an essential part of the way infants learn. When you see a baby banging away at something without apparent reason or logic, that odd little creature may well be testing hypotheses based on something that's surprised them (which is pretty much everything).

Researchers noticed that if babies saw a ball appearing to pass through a wall, they would test the ball's solidity by banging it on a table. If they saw a ball appearing to hover in midair, they tested the ball's response to gravity by dropping it. Surprise was the catalyst for curiosity and learning.

Surprise also drives behaviour change. New information needs to be reconciled with our existing beliefs and behaviours. *Cognitive dissonance* is the uncomfortable tension caused by wrangling two conflicting points of view. We can alleviate the mental discomfort by justifying our existing behaviours and discarding the new information, or by changing our behaviours to reflect the new knowledge.

So what does this all look like at work? Well, when it comes to behaviour change, there are few more challenging scenarios than safety. For some perverse reason, we won't change to save ourselves — literally. Which makes our next story all the more surprising.

## Zora sacrifices watermelons for the sake of safety

Day after day on a high-rise building site can be a repetitive affair. Every floor is the same as the one below, and construction often takes years to complete. But although the work is highly repetitive, each day, each floor and each season comes with a unique set of challenges. Staying alert and aware of potential risks is absolutely imperative to ensuring an incident-free site.

Group HSE Manager Zora knew that something needed to be done to keep people's focus on the potential hazards, including the consequences of objects falling from height.

The watermelon experiment wasn't new, but it hadn't been done on Zora's sites before. The experiment involved dropping a small object (like a block of wood) from a one-storey height onto a watermelon with and without a hard hat on. A glorious, highly educational abuse of fruit.

(continued)

**Zora sacrifices watermelons for the sake of safety** (continued)

The experiment worked on a couple of levels. Firstly, it did safety differently, which came as a surprise to many involved.* There was something undeniably exciting about watching a watermelon explode. The second benefit was what people learned from the experiment. Actually seeing the damage a falling block of wood could do, and witnessing first-hand how a hard hat could save someone's life, came as a real surprise to some.

The tests were captured in slow motion on people's phones and shared on the central intranet. For the bargain investment of a dozen watermelons and half an hour of people's time, Zora created a surprising experience that delivered a valuable lesson, one that would stick in people's minds and lead to safer behaviours.

* A word of warning: Suggesting something different will be met with resistance by those against trying anything new. Be ready for it! Research, case studies — heck, even this book — can all help justify your methods.

## A love/hate relationship

So is surprise always a good thing?

Not necessarily. Humans have a love/hate relationship with surprise. We're comfortable with routine, but we tend to become bored when life is too predictable. Surprise wakes us up. It's exciting, exhilarating and heightens our emotions. Yet it can also make us really uncomfortable.

Psychologists Tania Luna and LeeAnn Renninger found that surprise amplifies whatever emotion follows it by around 400 per cent. This makes it extremely powerful, but also makes it critical that we ensure the response is positive.

The challenge is that our tolerance for surprise varies, and this tolerance can be contextual to the individual at any moment in time. Our response can be based on past negative experiences. It may also be that we're experiencing too much uncertainty in our lives already, and surprise amplifies our existing anxiety.

This means using surprise discerningly **Surprise wakes us up. It's exciting, exhilarating and heightens our emotions.** in times of organisational upheaval or change. When people are already on edge and change-fatigued, even a positive surprise can become the final proverbial straw.

## A matter of timing

Timing is critical to maximise the impact of a surprise. *When* we deliver a surprise makes a big difference to how people respond.

Research on peak-end theory in customer service experiences shows that people are happiest when an experience begins as expected but finishes with a surprise. This is equally applicable to employee experiences. Considering an event, program or onboarding experience, we're likely to see a better return on investment if we begin fairly typically and save any surprises for key moments in the middle or right at the end.

Another important consideration is allowing time after a surprise for people to make sense of what happened. Failing to properly assimilate surprising or unfamiliar experiences can result in confusion, leading to avoidance or disengagement. Neither of which is ideal.

## SHOCK!

So what about shock?

Physiologically, shock is pretty darn similar to surprise, except it elicits a more sudden and intense negative emotional response. Oh yes, if our chapter title, 'Surprise!', gets an exclamation mark, 'SHOCK!' is worthy of capitalisation (if not the vulgarity of multiple exclamation marks).

Perhaps the most important difference, though, is that while surprise can delight, shock most certainly does not. It's often disturbing and typically confronting. It uses content that intentionally startles, terrifies, repulses, saddens, angers or offends the audience by violating norms, morals, values or traditions, or presenting the truth in its rawest form.

Advertising occasionally uses shock to cut through the typical fluffy advertising to capture attention and create conversation. Controversy, too. The *any publicity is good publicity* trope applies perfectly to this type of messaging. For this reason, shock has been the staple of charities, health and safety messaging, social causes and anti-everything campaigns for decades.

But does it work?

There's been plenty of debate about the effectiveness of this type of messaging, but the general consensus is that shock seizes our attention, significantly increases our awareness of an issue, and stays lodged in our memory longer than positive messages. Yet it has also been proven to be relatively ineffective at changing our behaviours.

In a PRWeek/OnePoll survey, 47 per cent of the public claimed that shocking images and stories didn't make them more likely to donate or support a cause. The National Society for the Prevention of Cruelty to Children in the UK found that their hardest-hitting campaigns were their least successful in terms of generating donations.

So why is shock so effective at grabbing our attention yet, unlike surprise, much less so at changing our behaviours?

Well, there's our *positivity bias* for starters. This is our tendency to believe negative outcomes won't happen to us. While young folk are particularly convinced they're bulletproof, all of us are prone to assuming that bad things only happen to other people.

Another problem is *selective perception* (*perceptual defence*, in particular). This is our tendency to focus on specific details while subconsciously ignoring everything else. Smokers are more prone to blocking out shocking anti-smoking messaging because they hit far too close to home. Just as professional drivers are more likely to tune out road safety messaging.

Finally, like any strategy that relies on our attention, using shock regularly can lead us to becoming desensitised and habituated.

## A question of anticipation versus surprise

In some instances, we need to weigh whether to sacrifice surprise (or shock) in favour of anticipation. This is perfectly illustrated in storytelling, where effective narratives often shun surprise by revealing information early. It works especially well when there's a dramatic or emotional revelation.

*A pair of star-cross'd lovers take their life…*

From the very beginning of Shakespeare's *Romeo and Juliet* we're told not to expect a happy ending. But that knowledge doesn't ruin the story. Forgoing surprise in favour of anticipation allows our emotions to build and makes our reaction to the finale even stronger.

Horror movies often use anticipation to build tension and amplify scary moments, and surprise to bring us relief (albeit a bloody and terrible type of liberation). Musical cues let us know something bad is about to happen, but it's only after the suspense has been drawn out to breaking point that they finally deliver the 'surprise'.

[*Cue suspenseful music…*]

# How to speak...
# surprise

### Idea #07: Deliver the unexpected

Effective surprises happen when we break people's expectations in a positive way. It doesn't need to be a big old wrecking ball of a surprise coming out of the blue; the smallest surprises can be the most memorable.

To deliver the unexpected, we can:

- Ensure a better outcome than was expected.

- Help people achieve things they didn't believe themselves capable of.

- Take a typical medium, message or experience and deliver it in an entirely new way. The least likely moments have the greatest potential to surprise and delight.

- Allow people the opportunity to change their own behaviours by using surprise to cause cognitive dissonance.

## Idea #08: Choose the right moment

Delivering the unexpected is great, but what's even better is delivering the unexpected when it's least expected. Surprise is all about timing.

This is by no means a rallying call to bring surprise into all we do. No, let's not start hiding in the hallways for sneaky water-cooler peekaboos. Let's not throw curve balls into every delivery with reckless abandon. Not only does that completely contradict the notion of a surprise, but it risks getting very old, really quick.

To deliver surprise at the right moment, we can:

- Save it for when we need attention most, to prevent it becoming predictable.

- Use surprise in the middle of the experience to create a memorable moment, or at the end to finish on a high.

- Allow time afterwards for people to make sense of their feelings.

- Avoid using it during times of unrest, upheaval or change.

- Find opportunities to use a combination of anticipation and surprise.

- Reward people for their contributions and performance.

## Idea #09: Commit to being shocking

To state the obvious, using shock effectively means being shocking. Doing it right guarantees a deluge of complaints, offence and general outrage. You know, all the things we generally try to avoid at work. For those without the stomach for confrontation, shock is not the method for you. Far better to use surprise instead.

For those with the fortitude to commit to being shocking, we can:

- Push it as far as possible. This isn't the time for fear or subtlety — it needs to be raw and powerful to be effective.

- Use explicit or confronting imagery, language and stories. Remember, we're looking to evoke a strong emotion. Disgust, anger, fear, sadness — these are the signs of a successful shock campaign.

- Make it as relatable as possible. We need to push past our positivity bias. Use real people and real stories for authentic emotions and reactions. Peers, friends or family have a greater impact than strangers or unfamiliar contexts. This is the only time it's appropriate to *not* leave the kids out of it.

- Highlight the emotional consequences, and how it might affect family and friends.

- Follow up with additional positive messaging focusing on the triggers rather than consequences, the result of change and a clear process for transformation. Shock is best used for attention and awareness campaigns, not for actually changing behaviours.

# Visual

## The sensory superiority of visual

At the time of writing, the internet is losing its collective mind over the revelation that Skittles are actually ALL THE SAME FLAVOUR. I bloody know, right! It turns out it was cheaper to vary the colour and smell than produce different flavours. Which means none of us have ever really tasted the rainbow. There is no lemon, there is no grape, there is only the deceptions of dishonest eyeballs (and nostrils).

It isn't the lies we've lived with all this time that give us the shivers. No, what thrills us is the power our visual system has to influence our perspective.

It's no surprise. Of all our senses, sight is the one we use most to understand our world. It's estimated that more than 90 per cent of the information we process is visual; and around 70 per cent of our receptors and roughly half our grey matter are dedicated (directly or indirectly) to dealing with it. In contrast, only around 8 per cent of our brain is dedicated to touch, and a meagre 3 per cent is focused on hearing. True story (until disproven, as is often the way with science).

This bias towards visual means a swag of benefits to appealing to people's eyes at work. Simplifying complex content, improving comprehension, increasing reaction times, aiding recall, attracting and directing our attention—these are the advantages of making communication visual.

Yet, perversely, the visual element of communication is quite often treated as an afterthought at best or decoration at worst. Oh yes, it's time for one of our fondest rants. [*Awkwardly drags heavy timber soapbox to centre of stage*]

Friends, there's a prevailing sense of indifference towards visual design. A belief that it's a frivolous waste of time and money. Perhaps it's a simple misconception that art and design are the same, despite their having very different purposes.

Full disclosure: we love art. When we stood captivated by Monet's *Water Lilies* for the very first time, we wept enough tears to fill a lily pond. But art for the sole sake of beauty has little relevance to us at work. Good design, on the other hand, does far more than decorate. Yessir! Visual design combines creativity with science to improve experiences, readability, usability, legibility, comprehension and connection. It simplifies. It makes messages memorable. It gains attention, increases engagement and makes a difference. All of which makes visual design very important indeed.

## Visuals appeal to our eyeballs

Spoiler alert: over the next few pages we take a solid swing at PowerPoint, a medium never intended to be used as a Word document in landscape orientation, but rather as a presentation platform to support the speaker visually. This ferocity extends to any wasted opportunity to use visual well. Because, when used effectively, visual inexorably attracts our attention and holds it. The simplicity allows us to consume content voraciously at a single glance.

## Visual fosters connection

Visualising content improves our connection to the content. It attracts our eyes, ensnares our minds and stays lodged in our memory long afterwards. It can make even the blandest data infinitely more palatable. Oh yes, when we push beyond the comfortable familiarity of words and visualise our content, the results can be quite thrilling.

## Visual builds recognition

Using visual to identify and differentiate is obvious when we consider external branding. We see a swoosh and know it's Nike; we know it stands for greatness and is synonymous with sport. Inside our organisations, building advocacy for our programs, departments or events benefits from the same branding techniques. Hold up though, champ. This isn't about dropping every document onto the corporate letterhead or painting everything from the same palette. We need to ... *differentiate*. [*Cue internal comms sirens*]

## Stephan and the ace up his sleeve

Analyst Stephan had quite the challenge. How to get a workforce enthusiastic and knowledgeable about his organisation's very crucial but also very dense global Key Performance Indicators (KPIs), data element definitions and job type definitions. Critical stuff, certainly, but weighing in at 137 pages, it wasn't what you'd consider a riveting read.

Stephan refused to believe this needed to be the case, though. He knew there must be a better way to communicate this bland but crucial information. A cheat sheet, of sorts, that gave busy folk a way to quickly find the information they needed, without putting them to sleep in the process.

The result? The Metrics Manual Cheat Cards, a deck of 52 cards containing short definitions and the opportunity for more card puns than you could ever hope to deal with. *Deal* with ... Ahh, yes.

Apart from the short definitions, the cards were primarily visual. Each of the three types of definitions was colour coded to make them easy to identify. A unique icon for each metric showed the purpose of the definition at a glance, as well as the relationships between similar metrics.

After dealing the cards to the relevant players, there wasn't a poker face to be seen (☺). The visual simplicity captured the attention of the people who needed to use them, and ensured that important metrics were gathered and reported when required.

## In the blink of an eye

The success of Stephan's Metrics Manual Cheat Cards came from transforming a text-dense document into highly visual form. While text is a grand choice for detail, the average punter lacks enthusiasm for girthy tomes of knowledge. Visualising content is a way to trim the fat — distilling complex content into simple, unambiguous imagery.

Someone once said that a picture is worth a thousand words, and that sure is a lot of words to be spared. Although that idiom smells suspiciously unscientific, it's been proven that we process images at truly shocking speeds.

Neuroscientists at MIT found that we can process entire images in as little as 13 milliseconds, and it's estimated that it takes only an additional 100 milliseconds to begin assigning meaning to them. To put that number in perspective, it takes us 300–400 milliseconds to blink.

In comparison, our eyes crawl through text at a pitiful rate, tediously scuttling over individual words before laboriously picking them up and grouping them together in comprehensible sentences and paragraphs.

Perhaps it's a matter of evolution. While text appeared only a few thousand years ago, visual's been keeping us alive since back when the survival of our species depended on immediately identifying a Tyrannosaurus as belligerent and a Brontosaurus as far less ornery.

We recognise these things visually long before we learn the language to describe them. It's probably just as well. *Tyrannosaurus* sure seems like an unnecessarily long name to give a murderous lizard. Best hope your companions have seen it and are already running by the time you spit that one out.*

Perhaps closely related to our penchant for not becoming dinner is our attraction to moving objects. Luca Cian, a Marketing professor at the University of Virginia's Darden School of Business, found that even a static image with the impression of movement can grab our attention earlier and improve our reaction time.

In one study, Cian explored how adding movement to the symbols used on road signage could improve driver reaction time. He found that the slightest tweak — to depict the figures running

* Never let chronology get in the way of a good story.

instead of walking—was enough to improve reaction time by around 50 milliseconds. That mightn't sound like much, but for a car travelling at 96.5 kilometres per hour, it's a stopping distance of 1.4 metres. Enough to prevent an accident or save a life.

Visualising content also helps us remember it.

Amy Poremba, an associate professor of Psychology and Neuroscience at the University of Iowa, discovered that we're much more likely to recall things we see (and touch) than things we hear. This difference becomes more pronounced over time.

Visual also trumps text when it comes to memory. Research into the *Picture Superiority Effect* reveals that when we read information, we remember about 10 per cent of it three days later. But if the same information includes a relevant image, our recall shoots up to a far more respectable 65 per cent. This is largely to do with how and where we process memories. Words are processed in short-term memory, whereas visuals are processed in long-term memory.

It's not just shapes and objects we remember either—colour aids recall too. Research out of Xerox found that simply adding colour to technical documents improves recall by up to 82 per cent.* This makes it a pretty safe decision to spray-paint any and all important messaging fluoro yellow, with a splash of neon orange for good measure.

**Although that idiom smells suspiciously unscientific, it's been proven that we process images at truly shocking speeds.**

## Turning data human

So what about data?

The mere mention sparks a tepid stock image of a spreadsheet filled with excessively decimal-pointed numbers, pie charts with primary-coloured slices and uninspiring titles—preceding a powerful urge to nap.

We don't blame you.

---

* Take this one with a grain of salt, pals. It's a suspiciously excellent statistic coming out of a company that sells colour printers and photocopiers.

Still, it's an important and unavoidable part of our work. Business performance and progress are tracked against targets, metrics and measurables. These are the benchmarks to which people are held accountable. And in an increasingly uncertain and volatile landscape, data offers a warm sense of certainty. A solid foundation for making decisions and setting direction.

It's serious business, but just because we're talking about statistics doesn't make this maths. It isn't folly to imagine data could be thrilling, that it could grab attention. We simply need to do it right.

Let's begin by simplifying. We're humans, not machines; parsing large quantities of data is not what we naturally do. For most of us (statisticians, mathematicians and researchers excluded), pulling the data back to what matters helps us focus, eases cognitive burden and increases the chance of retention.

Even the blandest statistics can be made more interesting by adding personality to the imagery.

Consider a metric like water conservation. Why does it need to be shown as a generic percentage or bar graph when it could be represented as a water drop, a dam or a lake?

Even better, let's make data relevant and relatable. Let's go beyond generic numbers and consider what means something to humans. This might mean comparing water usage at a plant to the number of showers typically taken in a year. Suddenly that big, meaningless number becomes something we can all relate to more easily.

Best of all, we can connect data to an emotion.

We can use visual metaphors or weave data into a narrative. Extending our previous example, we could document the journey of water as if it were a person. This transforms it from a commodity into a character we have a connection to—one we're far more likely to care about.

**It isn't folly to imagine data could be thrilling, that it could grab attention. We simply need to do it right.**

Collision rates are important benchmarks, but we could also represent them as the number of people in our team likely to be involved in accidents each month. This hits far closer to home than a heartless decimal point.

## Brandon plays with care

One of the world's leading toy manufacturers knows what it stands for—its vision and values revolve around *play*. Yet this value had never translated into safety. Nothing surprising about that; safety is serious business! But Brandon, Global Director of EHS, believed it was possible to 'play with care'.

Brandon had a vision of introducing an entirely new way of thinking about safety to a workforce that had never been asked to take an active role in safety before. His approach was multilayered. He wanted to engage managers in the behaviours and conversations needed to bring his Play with Care strategy to life, and he needed to do it in a way that required minimal translation for a workforce that spanned 12 languages.

He didn't hold back. Brandon took a highly visual approach to creating content that spanned cultures, languages, ages and abilities. He implemented tactics including a *Play with Care* journal to guide managers through the strategy. The journal incorporated slapstick comic illustrations to identify critical risks. It used visual activities such as safety hazard spot the differences and Where's Wally style puzzles to introduce key safety areas. It included visual guides to make safety interactions easy. And, to bring safety data to life, he used infographics with pictograms to ensure comprehension.

From the moment managers were introduced to Brandon's Play with Care strategy, they understood what it was about and what they needed to do. The success of tactics like the journal came from delivering key messages in a highly visual way. At first glance, it was simply a safety journal; nothing out of the ordinary there. But diving between the covers, the comics and interactive content were unlike anything the managers had experienced before.

## Differentiation, and a little defiance

So we're doing it—we're making it visual. Now we need to make it different. Heck, if we're after attention and impact, the last thing we want is our communication blending in with everything else.

We need to use novelty, unpredictability and the unexpected to drive curiosity and surprise. To cut through the typical corporate communication clutter, we need to set our work apart visually.

A word of warning, folks: at this stage it's worth mentioning that nothing, *nothing*—NOTH-ING—sounds the alarms of marketing and internal comms faster than talking about changing the visual style, or as they would say, 'tampering with The Brand'.

In some organisations, just thinking about using a fun font or a fruity colour palette will earn you a stern email with a style guide (or brand book) attached. These magical guidelines stipulate all the things you can and cannot do with the company brand. And they work wonderfully for ensuring external consistency. Unfortunately, using them internally with the same dogmatic enthusiasm for uniformity leads to everything looking exactly the same (more on that in *Beware: the insidious fog of habituation*, coming up next).

So if we want to differentiate, is there any place for consistency in our communication?

Sure there is, but not in the typical branding sense. It's not about ruthlessly conforming everything to *look* exactly the same. In fact, let's not even use the b-word [*whispers: 'brand'*]. That carries too many connotations and attracts unnecessary attention. Instead, let's call it... building *recognition*.

When it comes to recognition, we need consistency in our message, our values, our mission, our purpose—and in the level of care and effort put into our communication. These are the things that matter. And this is where we mention that there are two breeds of corporate comms people.

The first are the ones who get it. They understand that communication is about connection. They realise that style guides are *guides*, not law. We hope you're lucky to have these good folk in your organisation. You won't find any trouble there.

Then, though, there's the second breed. These are the people who believe that communication exists to be ruthlessly standardised. They believe in banging every triangle into a square. They believe that the style guide was put on Earth for the sole purpose of preaching it with great fervour to the masses, and anyone found guilty of bending The Rules must be punished.

You can spot the second type easily: they'll be the ones bellowing 'CONSISTENCY!' at every piece of collateral that slides across their desk. They'll be the ones red-penning every piece of communication with notations like 'Brand Guidelines! Page 148! …'.

**We need to use novelty, unpredictability and the unexpected to drive curiosity and surprise. To cut through the typical corporate communication clutter, we need to set our work apart visually.**

Here be monsters …

## Leena swims upstream

Leena heads up People, Leadership and Culture for a utilities company in a major city. She's great at her job, and genuinely wants to make a difference to the people working for her organisation.

Leena's company was going through a period of transformation. It was a turbulent time: the entire industry was changing, and restructures (read: downsizing) were happening across every department. Yes, cactus plants were being packed sadly into cardboard boxes and the halls were filled with forlorn folk doing the long, last walk. Trust was low, morale even lower.

There was a dire need to steer people through this transition period, and Leena saw the opportunity to improve people's experience by increasing transparency and delivering consistent information in a timely way.

With the help of her team, she put together a carefully considered framework along with a strategic comms plan. This provided the information, support and vision people desperately needed. It was no impersonal, jargon-heavy corporate document either. No, Leena put it together in a human way. And it shone like a beacon through the impersonal style of the other initiatives doing the rounds. Rich in visual metaphors, visionary roadmaps, hand-drawn videos — it was a triumph of speaking human …

(continued)

**Leena swims upstream** (continued)

And the Internal Communications department completely tore it apart.

They ravaged it down to the use of capitals and the exact font size and weight for headlines. The illustration style violated the explicit need for all images to be photos of water, so it was farewell to the visual metaphor. Only when every last drop of human had been stripped out did they stop and rebuild it to the exact specifications contained in the style guide.

By the time they'd finished, it looked exactly like every other piece of communication, and landed with an equal lack of enthusiasm and impact. It completely failed at making a difference, because it neglected to consider the needs of the intended audience.

This story doesn't have a completely unhappy ending, though.

Fast forward a couple of years and Leena was rebuilding her department and engaging the entire organisation in a culture change program. The difference this time? Evidently a few important battles had been won. Internal Comms had seen the need to put their style guide through some serious cosmetic surgery. Gone was the overly prescriptive, hello to possibility. The new guidelines allowed for greater flexibility and more variation.

Leena's work was glorious, but even more marvellous was the way it connected and the difference it made.

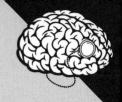

# How to speak...
# visual

### Idea #10: Make it visual

By bringing more visual to our communication, we can simplify content, reduce the amount of text required, improve comprehension, improve reaction times and aid recall. Where words can be misinterpreted, the right visual conveys a clearer and less ambiguous message. This is particularly important for global organisations, where visual transcends language and literacy barriers.

To make it visual, we can:

- Support important content with relevant illustrations, photos or diagrams.

- Translate important or complex information into diagrams or models. Just remember to keep it human by injecting personality, character, curiosity and humour.

- Use colour for impact and to aid recall, as well as differentiating or categorising information.

- Use dynamic images with a sense of movement when we need people to react quickly.

## Idea #11: Humanise data

There's no need for brain-numbing tables or flavourless pie charts, friends. Let's win eyeballs, hearts and minds by putting the human into data and visualising it better.

To humanise data, we can:

- Take it beyond the typical generic charts and graphs. We can use symbols, icons and imagery to visually represent what the data is about.

- Connect the figures, numbers or data points to a visual metaphor or narrative to evoke emotion.

- Make the data personal, relatable and relevant. Connect meaningless impersonal figures to more familiar statistics or real stories.

## Idea #12: Set it apart

We can use novelty to elicit curiosity and surprise to draw attention. And, we can do it with the minimum of trouble from even the most tyrannous corporate comms and marketing police.

To set it apart, we can:

- Use a different colour palette from typical communication. Most (good) brand guidelines specify a primary colour and several secondary colours. A lot of the time, communication is so standardised that only one or two colours are used frequently, leaving the rest of the branding rainbow ours to legitimately exploit.

- Choose a different style of imagery. There are almost infinite illustration and photography styles that we can use to set our work apart.

- Vary the medium and channel of communication. We're not constrained to posters, email or intranet; let your imagination run wild. In no brand guideline, ever, have we found carrier pigeons explicitly forbidden. Think on it…

- Avoid templates for important messaging. We get it, they save time, effort and a whole lot of angst from comms departments—but they also make everything look exactly the same, and that makes them blend in with everything else. If it's important, we need to create it from scratch.

- Change the tone of the headlines, captions and copy. Just like images, language can also set our communication apart.

## Idea #13: Build recognition

Our definition of *consistency* is to produce work that consistently wins attention, engages and influences. Our aim is for people to recognise where a piece of communication comes from, and immediately know it's worthy of their time.

To build recognition, we can:

- Stay flexible with the visual elements to keep people's attention. Change the colour, change the font, change the image style, change the channel or change the medium. Keep small visual links (perhaps just a colour or image style) between collateral to build recognition, without everything looking the same.

- Stay rigid with the things that matter: our core message, vision, values, purpose and mission. These are the foundations and filters for our communication.

# Beware...
## The insidious fog of habituation

In *The Art of War*, Sun Tzu proposes you know your enemy. Who are we to argue with Sun Tzu? So let's introduce you to yours. It isn't *attention* — that's the glorious spoils of victory. No, your enemy, your nemesis, the Brutus to your Caesar, is a phenomenon known as *habituation*.

Habit-you-what-now?

Oh, you might not have heard of it, but you've definitely felt it. If you've ever sat at the wheel of a car without remembering the details of the drive, lived below a flight path without noticing the planes passing overhead, found yourself able to conduct a perfectly normal conversation with other parents amid the chaos of a five-year-old's birthday party, or found yourself zoning out while ads are playing on television, you, my friend, have been habituated.

Far more relevant to us, though, is the impact of habituation on communication.

The real enemy to seizing attention is located right inside our brains, and the way they're wired to filter out the familiar. Which makes understanding — and beating — habituation very important indeed.

### It's all in our minds

Because we're the type that likes to pulls things apart to see how they work, let's take a metaphorical scalpel to skull and show you the innards.

Inside our brains are two minds: implicit and explicit. They work together, but don't completely understand each other. Like an elderly couple, a horse and rider, or, in the delightfully everyman lingo of kc7wbq on Reddit, 'Lizard and Big Daddy':

> *Your mind is made up of two minds. You have the big daddy who is you and your conscious thoughts. He's slow, but very smart. Then you have your lizard brain. He's not so smart, but he's fast. He's the guy that catches a ball thrown at your face. Your big daddy brain likes to think about new things and big things. Once he starts to get bored he likes to pass tasks off to the lizard brain. This is called forming a habit, or learning a skill. When you first started to learn to drive a car, or travel a new road, your big daddy brain had to pay attention to make decisions and control your muscles. But now you've driven so much your lizard brain knows how to do it. If your big daddy brain wants to monitor what your lizard brain does that's okay, and probably good from a safety point of view, but it's not necessary any more.*

To summarise with a little less dramatic flair, our implicit mind takes care of the routine tasks, the things that can be done automatically, freeing the explicit mind to think about other things. These are big thoughts, or daydreams even—our explicit mind freewheeling until the unexpected occurs. Surprise, shock or curiosity—these all snap our explicit mind back to attention.

The curious relationship between these two minds is the reason we can perform common tasks with very little conscious thought. And this makes repetitive jobs particularly prone to habituation. Factory work, routine office work, construction, driving—these are roles where habituation is most likely to occur, and where people are most likely to be on autopilot.

**Surprise, shock or curiosity—these all snap our explicit mind back to attention.** By now you might be wondering, why are our brains so hell-bent on blocking our attention? What possible purpose could habituation serve?

Well, it comes down to survival, and one inescapable truth…

## We're all animals

Here's a potentially confronting fact: no matter the couture we drape our hairless hides in, the literature we read, or our proficiency at assembling a cheese and charcuterie board—we're all just animals. And we have a few things in common with every other beast that roams this world—notably, a will to survive, and the ability to learn in order to survive.

This way of learning is habituation.

Over time, we learn not to respond to something that happens repeatedly without change, reward or punishment. This allows us to tune out the non-essentials and to focus fully on the things that matter—the things that really demand our attention.

Picture a young deer out in the woods. A sudden noise—a pine cone falling, perhaps—and the deer is startled! Ahh...but over time and many pine cones later, provided one doesn't land on its head, the noise no longer startles the deer.

Then there's communication at work.

Now, we're fairly confident in assuming that the most critical injury ever inflicted by corporate comms was probably a paper cut, and the only fatality—death by PowerPoint. This places typical corporate communications low in our hierarchy of needs, and therefore less worthy of our attention.

Yes, Big Daddy just left the building; the Lizard's in charge.

But how does it work exactly, and, more importantly, how do we beat it?

## It's a matter of exposure

The speed at which habituation occurs depends on four main factors:

1. *Frequency*: The more often we're exposed to something, the faster habituation occurs.

2. *Interval*: The less time between exposures to something, the faster habituation occurs.

3. *Duration*: The longer we're exposed to something, the faster habituation occurs.

4. *Strength*: The stronger something is, the faster habituation occurs. But here's a catch: exposure to *very* strong stimuli results in slower habituation, and in extreme cases it may never occur at all.

Now, consider how most organisations communicate: a constant bombardment of calls, memos, posters, intranet announcements, meetings and emails by the million. And when design is involved, reach for the style guide; copy and paste.

High frequency, short interval, long exposure and high consistency—the perfect framework for habituation.

Yes, communicating with our people using the same methods and mediums, exactly the same language, tone and visual style, day in and day out, causes communication to become like the backgrounds of our daily commute—blurring by, blotted out.

Fortunately, most of the strategies contained in this book are proven habituation-breakers. Curiosity, anticipation, surprise, humour, visual—these are some of the ways we cut through habituation to win people's attention.

We can also break habituation by attacking the causes.

## Build a rhythm of unpredictability and delight

Change the stimulus, change the frequency, change the interval, change the duration, tone down the strength—these things break habituation.

We need to mix it up.

Change the medium, change the channel, change the style. If you always use posters, share a video. If you use video for everything, plaster the toilet doors with a poster or two. If safety posters have been gathering dust since mutton-chops were fashionable, tear them down and change them up. Never default to templates for the really important stuff.

It's good to build rituals and establish routine, but never let them fade into predictable. Instead, build a rhythm of unpredictability and delight.

Consistency, consistency, consistency — grenade.

## Shred the style guide

Words quite simply fail us when it comes to expressing the absurdity of external brand guidelines being used for internal communication, so we'll borrow the words of Robin Williams from *Dead Poets Society*:

> *Excrement. That's what I think of [style guides]. We're not laying pipe. We're talking about poetry... Now, I want you to rip out that page. Go on... Rip!... Rip it out!... We'll perforate it, put it on a roll. It's not the Bible... You're not gonna go to Hell for this.*

Somewhere out there in fluoro-lit cubicles, certain comms teams are all a-tremble. Someone just said a bad, bad thing.

We do feel the tiniest bit terrible for saying it. Design and branding is an integral part of our company's DNA, so we wage war on style guides with a heavy heart. One half admiring the perfection of their consistency, the depth of their detail. The other half aware that for communicating internally, they are fundamentally flawed.

**It's good to build rituals and establish routine, but never let them fade into predictable. Instead, build a rhythm of unpredictability and delight.**

The problem is in their purpose. Brand guidelines are made to foster highly consistent communication, intended to strip out variation. Frequency, interval, duration, strength. These factors work extremely well to gain the attention of our customers, folk who are exposed to our branding and communication intermittently. But when we use the same techniques internally, to people exposed to the branding every single day...

Hello, habituation.

Unfortunately, the typical process in many organisations is to finish a job and send it to comms for approval. Here, folk who've studied Marketing and Branding do exactly what they've been taught and hired to do: standardise and conform. They run the style guide, sweat the detail, make it consistent. And, unintentionally—dip it invisible.

Once we're habituated, it's farewell attention—which is actually a success of sorts, because you can bet all further communication will be consistently ignored.

**They run the style guide, sweat the detail, make it consistent. And, unintentionally—dip it invisible.** Effective communication in the workplace should consider more than the detail, more than the visual; it should focus on vision. The why. The culture. The values. The message. The stories. Without getting hung up on the precise leading for subheadings or the exact font weight for titles.

It should foster creativity; allow for variation. Let's push past typical; let's create something unique. Let's stop external branding for internal communication, selling to the already-sold. Heck, leave the logos off completely—we're quite sure everyone knows where they work.

Go ahead, dare to create communication that grabs attention and makes a difference. Dare to defy the style guide, and the people who blindly parrot it.

Rip! Rip! Rip it out...

# Narratives
## The titillations of a well-told tale

Our species has been telling tales since we first grunted indecent and hairy onto icy tundras, waving rocks at things much bigger and more ill-tempered than us. The lucky ones who made it home told stories of their survival to their tribe, and their tribe learned valuable lessons about bigger stones and better cardiovascular endurance.

From way back then, to now, and probably far into the future, storytelling is the way we naturally share and interpret experiences, pass on knowledge, record history and entertain one another. Yes, long before PowerPoint and policy manuals, stories were the way we learned things: skills, history, ethics, morals, cultural norms … and aforementioned wildlife evasion.

There's no way we could talk about speaking human without including narratives. But let's be frank, using stories in the workplace is hardly a groundbreaking idea. There are countless books, articles and experts in the industry spruiking storytelling as the cure to all our engagement troubles.

Intuitively, most of us already know that stories are a great way to connect. It's how and when we use them that trips us up. Not to mention that some of us are natural storytellers, and others … not so much. Don't worry, though, we don't need to become the type who tells 'the one that got away' fishing yarns down at the local pub on a Saturday night. The best business narratives are subtly woven into communication when we need to capture people's imagination and encourage them to get on board with complex concepts or strategies.

### Narratives bring ideas to life

We can use narratives to paint a vivid picture of what the journey from then to now to tomorrow might look like. This can include sharing a five-year department plan with the C-suite or introducing new technology that will change the way we'll work. We can also use narratives to create an overarching theme for material that would otherwise be quite mundane. This might be bringing a safety induction to life or using a metaphor for organisational change.

### Narratives change people's perspective

We can use narratives to share what we've learned from past experiences. Perhaps someone had a great idea that saved the company a ton of money. Maybe we ballsed something up and want to ensure it never happens again. We can also use narratives when we want people to see something from someone else's perspective. This might be sharing a story from a client's point of view to give a deeper understanding of the challenges they face.

### Narratives build cultures

We can use narratives to engage people in a common purpose. This might be rallying the entire organisation around the vision, or sharing stories that bring the values to life.

None of these narratives need to be complicated. They certainly don't need to be epic sagas. The most compelling stories are often right in front of us.

### Scarlett tells Ron's story

Aged care can be an extremely rewarding job, but it presents the challenge of working with people who are coming to terms with entering a new stage of their lives. This realisation can be daunting and scary, and lead to difficult interactions between carer and client.

Scarlett, the General Manager of a large aged care provider, realised that preparing her people for the realities of their roles was critical to providing quality care for clients, and a long and rewarding career for employees. She could have compiled a lengthy checklist of her expectations for dealing with clients, a list of do's and don'ts for people to learn. Instead, she shared a story of one particular client.

Ron is an 89-year-old man who had moved from London to be closer to his daughter for the final innings of his life. He had been a sports journalist once upon a time, and while he isn't so active these days, Ron still enjoys watching all sorts of sports on the telly, sometimes staying up till 3 am. Ron is also a fussy eater: he eats just two pieces of toast smothered in real butter for breakfast and refuses to drink anything except raspberry cordial.

Scarlett shared Ron's fears about moving into an aged care facility, and his daughter's fears for her father. She did all this by developing a first-person narrative, told by Ron himself.

Employees joining the company would watch the simple animated story, and afterwards they'd have a discussion about what 'person-centred care' meant for Ron. They discussed how they could fulfil their roles in challenging environments with the resources available. Then they'd brainstorm ideas on how they could really make Ron's day.

## Rallying the senses

Ron's story helped employees see situations from their clients' perspective. It also helped them connect with each other by sharing stories about their own parents or people they'd cared for previously.

So what is it about stories that fosters these types of interactions? Because poring over a checklist or technical manual rarely elicits the same level of engagement.

Well, inside that magnificent bone cavern you call a skull is a brain. Hopefully. And inside that brain are Broca's and Wernicke's regions, where all language is processed and meaning is assigned to words. Whenever our communication is laden with facts or logic, it's business as usual in these areas.

Narratives, however, shake things up. In addition to the language processing areas, stories stimulate other areas of our brain — areas typically associated with our senses. This is because, like life, stories tend to be rich in sensory detail.

*Bone-weary and slightly dejected, Frank fell into his favourite chair to shake off the day. He blew out a long breath, then reached for a board with a fresh loaf of ciabatta and a particularly pungent blue cheese.*

*Blue cheese.* The mere mention conjures a formidable aroma. But what really thrills is that in that split second while reading the word, we aren't exactly *imagining* the smell. Our brain actually responds as if we've taken a big old whiff.

Researcher Julio González and pals discovered that reading words associated with strong smells ('coffee', 'garlic' or 'jasmine') excites our primary olfactory cortex. Cognitive scientist Véronique Boulenger found that a sentence like 'Pablo kicked the ball' triggers activity in our motor cortex. This isn't just general activity either; the area of the cortex that's activated relates to the part of the body the sentence describes.

Folk from Emory University found that metaphors involving texture ('the singer had a velvet voice' or 'he had leathery hands') arouses our sensory cortex. In contrast, generic phrases with a similar meaning ('she had a pleasing voice' and 'he had strong hands') does not.

These studies show that our brain treats reading or listening to stories and metaphors involving our senses as if we were actually experiencing it. This makes communication laden with metaphors and sensory detail richer, more compelling and more memorable.

## A meeting of minds

Beyond stimulating our senses, a curious phenomenon occurs between storyteller and audience. A well-told tale evokes *neural entrainment*, which may sound like a sci-fi thriller but is actually a type of cognitive coupling where the listener's brain activity aligns with the speaker's.

Psychologist Uri Hasson conducted a series of experiments that revealed that the more we understand or relate to a story, the closer our brain activity aligns. This alignment goes beyond auditory and language cortices and into the higher order areas—the parts that deal with meaning.

To confirm his findings, Hasson had the story translated into Russian and played the recording to Russian speakers. As expected, activity in the auditory cortex was different from the English speakers, reflecting the difference in words. However, the higher order areas showed exactly the same activity as the English speakers. The story carried the same meaning and influence, no matter the language it was told in.

Hasson also found that the more the storyteller established shared context and common ground, the closer the listener's brain activity aligned. This explains why good storytellers intuitively bounce back and forth with their audience to identify similarities.

A fascinating by-product of this brain-bonding is our tendency to make other people's tales our own. When we hear a story, our first instinct is to relate it to our own experiences, stimulating a part of the brain called the insula, which associates memories with emotions. When we find something in the story we identify with, the lines between memory, story and reality begin to blur. We begin to experience the story as if it had actually happened to us.

Yes, if you've ever told someone a story then had it told back to you a few weeks later, fist bump for telling a truly excellent tale. Potential for awkwardness aside, it demonstrates the power of narratives to influence others. Perhaps it's one of the reason leaders with strong storytelling skills tend to be better at building rapport and gaining buy-in.

Imagine the possibilities for fostering this cognitive coupling in your work. Rather than turgid dumps of content, a simple story could give others ownership

**Rather than turgid dumps of content, a simple story could give others ownership of the idea or message, making it more likely they'll remember it and act on it.**

of the idea or message, making it more likely they'll remember it and act on it. This may sound a little like mind control, but unlike splitting the atom, we hope you'll use this knowledge for good.

## Emily and the unsung heroes

Fortunately for most of us, a stubbed toe or bruised ego will likely be the worst injury we'll suffer during our careers. But on the odd occasion things go properly south, it's lucky for the unlucky few that organisations like Emily's exist to help get them back to work afterwards.

Let's be honest (because: truth and transparency), this isn't glamorous work. It's admin-heavy and often thankless, yet for the folk who do it, it's also incredibly rewarding. There's a strong sense of pride in finding solutions to often complicated situations.

Emily, People and Culture Manager, was on a mission to develop an exciting employer brand that attracted the right people to her organisation. But it needed to be authentic about who and what the business was about. This isn't a workplace of foosball tables and slippery slides. It's floors of cubicles filled with dedicated folk quietly doing their work. The rowdiest it gets is the odd wry smile for the satisfaction of a job well done.

So Emily chose a narrative that spoke loudly to a quiet few. A call to the unsung heroes; not the Batmans, not even the Robins, but the Alfreds and Lucius Foxes. She wasn't looking for the type with a proclivity for capes and cavorting around being all gung-ho; she was after the quiet achievers.

She understood exactly the types of individual suited to working in her organisation, and she shared a simple narrative that spoke directly to them.

## Crafting compelling tales

Emily could have presented a logical list of all the ways a potential candidate would be a match. And no doubt she did. But presenting the information in the form of a narrative meant potential candidates could put themselves into the brand more easily and get a better sense of what it would be like to work there.

So if narratives are proven to be more influential than logic, why is most corporate messaging still short on story and fat with fact? There's certainly no shortage of workplace scenarios that can be turned into fascinating tales. Instead, we get ten dozen checklists, hundred-page Word documents and a thousand bullet points in PowerPoint.

We admit that, like toilet paper, PowerPoint has its purpose. Oh, but the ongoing abuse. Not the medium so much as its mind-numbing application. The detailed diagrams! The paragraphs of technical text! People speak of death by PowerPoint, but that would be sweet mercy compared with the torturous presentations dealt out in some organisations on a daily basis.

Fortunately, stories can be told in almost any medium. They can be visual, auditory, written or kinaesthetic. They can be shared as videos, books, posters, flyers, conversations, speeches, interpretive dance—heck, even PowerPoint, if used in place of the typical assault-by-bullet-point.

**So if narratives are proven to be more influential than logic, why is most corporate messaging still short on story and fat with fact?**

Stories certainly don't need to be complex to be engaging. The best tales often use simple language and a straightforward structure. The typical arc—from beginning, through a series of complications, to a climax and final resolution—has remained unchanged for centuries.

Students at Tufts University stole a little of Disney's pixie dust by discovering it's possible to map almost all their stories to exactly the same structure. Think back to the last one you watched: begins predictably, builds to a climax, concludes with a happy ending (not unlike date night, TBH).

This archetype is known as the *hero's journey*. It's a compelling template: a likeable hero (preferably an underdog) answers the call to adventure, embarks on a quest, overcomes obstacles, battles a villain and eventually wins the object of their desire (or fails, in bitter sweet tragedy).

It's a tale we've heard a million times through a seemingly inexhaustible array of executions and applications. From myth and legend, to entertainment, politics, branding and business. The hero's journey gives us the ideal narrative structure for anything from a reward and recognition program to a culture change program.

## Clive has a sweet idea

Encouraging people to take an active role in innovation can be a tough sell. Sticks and carrots can provide a short-term flurry of ideas and innovations, but inevitably people lose interest and fall back into business as usual. Don, Senior Health and Safety Manager at a manufacturing facility, tried a different approach. While searching for stories about people who'd gone above and beyond to solve problems that improved safety for everyone, he stumbled on this tale:

*Clive had been consumed by a problem at work. In his section, there were large sugar bags that needed lifting and loading into a bin. But because the bags were too heavy for one person to lift, Clive had to wait for someone else to help him. He'd given it a good crack a couple of times, and come close to becoming a manual handling statistic.*

*Then Clive had an idea: smaller, lighter sugar bags. Genius!*

*He went through the right channels and presented his plan. Head nods all round, and in no time at all Clive's idea had been implemented.*

Don translated this story into a simple one-page comic and included it in the employee magazine. Clive's story was the perfect example of everyone contributing to a safety culture, and Don encouraged others to keep on the lookout for similar stories to share.

# How to speak…
# narratives

### Idea #14: Share compelling stories

Let's bring more stories into our communication. These can be big, overarching narratives for programs, campaigns or brands. Or they can be smaller stories used in one-off applications.

Regardless of scale, to share compelling stories, we can:

- Keep them simple. We're looking for a singular idea or theme that can be told in various levels of detail, depending on the medium.

- Connect the narrative to our purpose and/or brand. It should reinforce the vision, values and driving emotions. It should support the outcome we're trying to achieve.

- Establish context. This allows people to inject themselves into the story, making it more engaging and influential.

- Use framing to determine how the story is interpreted.

- Include sensory details and use metaphors. Describe how things look, feel, sound, smell and taste. This triggers our senses and makes our stories richer and more compelling.

- Use narratives in learning applications to help others see situations from different perspectives.

## Idea #15: Tell the tale visually

While stories can be told in any medium, we're big advocates of sharing them visually. This combines the advantages of storytelling (emotion and influence) with the benefits of visualising content (ease and speed of consumption).

To tell the tale visually, we can:

- Use videos. These have the advantage of hitting us from visual and auditory angles. The medium allows us to tell rich stories in a multitude of styles, from animation to film. Animation (like comics) allows less literal depictions of sensitive content. Conversely, video of real people carries authenticity and forges connection.

- Use comics. These visual narratives allow us to create hyperreal scenarios and characters. We can exaggerate points in order to prove them, and create perfect personas without using real people or stock photography. Their non-literal nature allows people to insert themselves into the story more easily. They also tend to be less confronting in sensitive circumstances (consider the things done to the characters in children's Warner Bros cartoons).

- Use memes. The popularity of this medium comes from the way they communicate a story in a single frame. When we're up against short timeframes and even shorter attention spans, memes can be the ideal way to share our story.

# Emotions
## The paradoxical logic of getting emotional

Perhaps the most confusing, wonderful, infuriating, exciting, maddening, humorous, occasionally downright depressing part of being human is our emotions. Yes, each day it's all aboard a rollercoaster of feels for a thrillingly unpredictable ride through the highs and lows of life.

For a solid chunk of the 20th century, we were strongly encouraged to leave our emotions at home. Work was an eight-hour amnesty, an emotional Switzerland of sorts. Dammit, you go to work to do the business! How was anyone meant to make smart decisions if emotions turned up all illogical and irrational and ruined the day.

Fortunately, these beliefs have changed in most workplaces, or are in the process of changing in slower moving organisations. Studies have proven what the more emotionally savvy among us already knew intuitively: emotions are healthy in the workplace, provided they're well managed. More than healthy, actually. When woven into our working life, they're powerful intrinsic motivators of learning and behaviour.

### Emotions are lenses for our messaging

The strongest messages always appeal to emotions — seizing our hearts before seducing our minds. Our communication should consider how we want people to feel, as well as providing them with what they need to know. Let's leave bland, emotionless language behind and embrace all them feels.

### Emotions are precursors to behaviour

We can use positive emotions or negative emotions to influence behaviour. Since our survival instinct relies on our attention being drawn towards negative things, it's easy to default to negativity in our messaging. But *easy* doesn't equate to *better*. It's positive emotions that drive curiosity, learning, recall and long-term behaviour change. When it comes to influence, positivity trumps negativity every time.

### Emotions build connection

Like it or not, businesses are full of people, and people are full of emotions, making it paradoxically logical that we need to get better at dealing with feelings at work. The way we manage our own and others' emotions is critical to building better relationships.

## The curious relationship between words and feelings

Let's start by slipping into something a little less comfortable (your skull) for a brief physiological poke.

Emotions are born in our amygdala and passed through the limbic system via a network of neural pathways to the neocortex, where perception, reasoning, thinking and learning occur. These emotions are transmitted with a cue for how we should react physically. Anger primes us to fight and happiness makes us smile. In most cases, we have an opportunity to reflect on our feelings before we respond (a good thing, given the stupidity that often ensues when we act without thinking!).

Until relatively recently, emotions were an area of much debate and very little fact. How do you express intangible, complex, highly personal and difficult-to-define feelings in words? Fortunately, advances in brain imaging provided us with insights far less prone to differences in interpretation. And the resulting research uncovered a fascinating relationship between language and emotions.

Let's begin with the question: which comes first, words or feelings? Oho! It's the oft-used chicken-and-egg scenario here. But we'll roll with the well-worn and best-proven constructionist approach: language helps constitute emotion.

Various studies show that while we're experiencing an emotion, the language areas in our brain are active, even when we're not actually using words to express our feelings. This suggests that language does more than translate our feelings into words; it actually helps shape those emotions.

There's increasing evidence that we can consciously change the intensity, meaning and expression of our experience by using language to re-categorise our emotional state. In psychology, this is known as reappraisal.

Let's say we were quivering at the top of a diving board, paralysed by fear. We could re-categorise our feeling from 'terrified' to 'exhilarated'. Neuroimaging shows that when we do this, there's activity in our ventrolateral **But we'll roll with the well-worn and best-proven constructionist approach: language helps constitute emotion.** and dorsomedial prefrontal cortices, areas associated with semantic knowledge and retrieval. In plain human, language is playing a role in changing our emotion.

It's also possible to regulate our emotions simply by identifying them, using another psychology technique known as affect labelling.

Psychologists Pennebaker, Lieberman and pals showed research participants images of facial expressions revealing strong emotions. Using fMRI, they observed that the images elicited a strong response in the amygdala, an area associated with emotion—particularly fear. Interestingly, though, when participants were asked to label the emotion, activity in the amygdala decreased while it increased in the prefrontal cortical regions, where vigilance and discrimination occur. Naming their emotion turned the photos into an object of academic scrutiny, rather than a cause for fear.

Of course, if you regularly practise mindfulness, you're probably rolling your eyes right now. The concept of affect labelling certainly isn't confined to psychology, and it definitely isn't new. It's known by many names, and the fundamentals are used in numerous techniques.

In many forms of mindfulness, practitioners label their psychological state with a word. Feelings, senses and emotions are observed without judgement, and without trying to change or eliminate them. Not surprisingly, these forms of mindfulness produce exactly the same brain activity as affect labelling.

Whether it's mindfulness, psychology, acceptance commitment therapy, journaling or simply telling the kids to 'use your words!', it's proven that writing or talking about emotions can help reduce the intensity and decrease anxiety around them.

On a more lowbrow note, swearing not only effectively expresses our emotions, but also amplifies them. Oh yes, a good verbal ejaculation of filthy adjectives can actually intensify your feelings. Feeling joyous? Want to feel *more* joyous? Bellow a fiery 'FUCK YEAH!' and ride that post-profanity high.

You're welcome.

## Liam helps his team manage their emotions

Let's venture into the wilds and join the Field Sales team of the world's largest food and beverage company. A demographically diverse group, these are the folk tasked with the crucial role of delivering product to various stores, setting up point-of-sale displays and arranging stock.

Liam knew that working in Field Sales could be a stressful job. People were often out on their own in unpredictable environments, dealing with traffic, docks, retailers, the public—and always up against the clock. It's a job that goes from zero to hectic in a matter of seconds, which makes it important to stay alert and prepared for anything.

For the Field Sales team, staying safe both physically and mentally came down to staying in the moment and making smart decisions. And, often, focus was the difference between a safe and unsafe outcome.

The existing Field Sales induction material was serviceable, but Liam knew it could be more effective at setting up new recruits to work safely and efficiently. So he began by overhauling the induction process.

Instead of producing the type of instructional manual that's read once then cast aside, the Field Guide was designed as a journal that would be used daily, helping employees deal with the emotional rollercoaster that work could be. In addition to providing operational information, it incorporated mindfulness information, techniques, triggers and journaling activities to help the Field Sales team keep focused — and stay safe.

By considering the emotional impact of the job, Liam was able to design an induction program and collateral with a difference. A program that stood out from others because of its content, delivery and a relationship founded on empathy. A great basis for any working relationship.

## The allure of negative versus the power of positive

As well as supporting our teams emotionally, we can also use emotions to encourage learning and change behaviours.

To see how effectively emotions drive behaviour, we need only look to the advertising industry. These folk have been dominating that game for decades. Oh yes, they discovered that toying with our emotions is a very effective way of loosening the strings on our money bags.

Neuroscientist Antonio Damasio confirms that when it comes to decision making, feelings and emotions always dominate our cognition. fMRI scans of our brains show that when evaluating a piece of advertising, consumers respond emotionally first, proving we're emotional creatures, far more swayed by feels than facts.

**Feeling joyous? Want to feel *more* joyous? Bellow a fiery 'FUCK YEAH!' and ride that post-profanity high.**

Given some truly appalling purchase decisions (I'm looking at you, unnecessarily neon short shorts), it's a relief to discover that there's usually little logic in our decisions. We buy emotionally, then search for features, benefits and facts to justify our purchases (particularly foolish, frivolous, fluorescent ones).

So are some emotions more potent than others?

Oh yes, and there's no way to make the next part painless, so we'll peel the bandaid quick. We're generally fearful creatures with a predisposition to negativity. [*Winces*]

In psychology, this is known as the *negativity bias*. If we take two stimuli of equal strength, the negative one will affect us more in the moment than a neutral or positive one. This bias exists in attention, decision making, learning and memory.

The negativity bias makes sense from an evolutionary perspective. Fear is an excellent emotion for survival, especially when it comes to directing attention. Our tendency to be drawn towards things that previous experience indicates might be threatening—loud noises, violence, unpleasant images, creatures with unfriendly intentions—comes from a basic urge to survive.

Naturally, the more attention we direct toward something, the more likely it is that we'll learn and remember it. This self-flagellistic bent towards recalling negative experiences even leads us to underestimate how often we have positive experiences. Psychologist Rick Hanson sums it up nicely: 'the brain is like Velcro for negative experiences but Teflon for positive ones'.

Yes, it's no surprise we're glued to the train wreck that is reality television. We're compelled to watch the episode of our favourite drama where a much-loved character cashes their final cheque. And based on watching any current affairs program ever, it's obvious we also love to be the bearers (and recipients) of bad news. Which is unfortunate really, because our attitudes tend to be influenced more by bad news than good, and negativity is more contagious than positivity. Heck, it's even estimated that it takes us around five good interactions to make up for just one bad one. It's no wonder morale is tough to maintain in the workplace.

It's a vicious, vicious cycle, people! We need to break this sick relationship with negativity, not perpetuate it. Just because it's our default, doesn't make it good for us. And just because it's easy, doesn't make it effective.

Negative emotions may have an insidious impact on us, but as we discovered when looking at shock campaigns in 'Surprise!', they're not particularly effective at actually changing people's behaviour for the better. This isn't to say they can't; experiencing a negative event or fear of failure both have the capacity to change us, but positive emotions put us in a far better and more sustainable mindset.

The most effective learning, the most progressive thinking, the smartest decisions, the greatest resilience to setbacks — these all take place when we're curious and feeling positive towards the task.

Drawing on a decade of data, happiness researcher Shawn Achor found that a positive mind significantly outperforms a negative, neutral or stressed-out brain. His findings extended to intelligence, energy, resilience, the duration people stay committed to projects, open-mindedness, number of connections and health.

In a study presented at the American Association for the Advancement of Science, 44 doctors were each given hypothetical patient files containing a misdiagnosis from another hospital and asked to correctly identify the illness. Half the group were supplied with medical journals to review in advance. The other half were given a bag of goodies and appreciation for their participation. The result? The group who were primed for positive emotions reached the correct diagnosis twice as fast, and demonstrated three times more intellectual flexibility in reaching their conclusion. Sugar and satisfaction trumped knowledge alone.

**This self-flagellistic bent towards recalling negative experiences even leads us to underestimate how often we have positive experiences.**

Why? Well, remember that emotions come with a physiological cue for how we should respond. We briefly mentioned that anger prepares us to fight, which is great if we're being mugged, but not particularly helpful at work. Fury and other negative emotions rarely prime us to work together effectively. Positive emotions, however, tend to motivate curiosity, creativity, relationship building, playfulness, enthusiasm and resilience. All of which are very useful indeed when it comes to performance and promoting positive behaviour change.

## Zora and Randy foster care, courage and pride

Safety communication in the construction industry generally isn't a feel-good affair. The inherent hazards mean that messaging tends to focus on the risks associated with certain behaviours: *don't do that, or something bad will happen.* After years spent perfecting the systems, procedures and processes but still not seeing the results they wanted, Zora, Group HSE Manager, and Randy, Group Organisation Development Manager, decided to take a different approach.

They wanted to get away from the negative messaging and bad news stories used in typical safety communication, and build a safety culture on positive foundations. Their Building Safety Greatness program used the emotions of *Care, Courage* and *Pride* as the catalyst to change behaviours and, ultimately, shift their culture.

*Care* encouraged people to look out for each other, understanding what others' needs were on site, and caring enough to do the job right so everyone went home safely at the end of the day.

*Courage* was about being brave enough to ask questions, have the tough conversations and stop if something didn't seem quite right.

*Pride* was about not only finishing a project on time and on budget, but finishing it without incident.

The program was designed to increase awareness of the 'why' behind safety by engaging a greater number of people in more human interactions. Training, toolbox talks, site activations, challenges and traditional comms channels were all used to bring Building Safety Greatness to life.

The effectiveness of the program came from pushing safety beyond the safe and well-trodden path of systems, procedures, processes and negative messaging and bringing it back to a fundamentally human approach.

# How to speak…
# emotion

### Idea #16: Lead with emotion

Emotions are unavoidable, but that doesn't mean we can't influence them. We can use communication to educate and regulate emotions at work. Leading with emotion means taking an empathetic approach and designing experiences to support people's emotional journeys. People may struggle to remember our words, but they rarely forget how we make them feel.

To lead with emotion, we can:

- Make people feel something. There should be a driving emotion behind our message.

- Use metaphors and stories to evoke emotions. Facts, figures and detail can be used to back it up.

- Incorporate mindfulness techniques and information into communication. This gives people an opportunity to understand and manage their own emotions.

- Encourage people to talk about their emotions in the right ways, rather than fostering an environment where everyone pretends to become emotionless the moment they arrive at work.

- Evoke positive emotions. These are intrinsic motivators for curiosity, learning and behaviour change.

# Humour

## The serious business of being funny

Perhaps the biggest instigator of The Serious Conversation is suggesting humour at work. Yes, quite ironically, nothing gets some people more straight-faced than the thought of other people laughing.

We understand the fear. Humour can feel like a massive risk, especially when communicating a serious or sensitive topic. There's the concern of trivialising, making light or making fun of a situation that may be far from funny. The spectre of potential insult looms. There's also the legitimate fear of a joke falling flat. We've all seen what happens when humour takes a big ol' bellyflop from the high board. The impact is seldom pretty.

Let's allay those fears. There's a subtle but definite distinction between seeing humour around a situation, and making light of the message. Comedians walk that line every time they get up on stage. Advertising uses it frequently and very effectively. Let's trust that empathy will aid us in determining what's funny, and what's appropriate.

But why even risk it?

Well, research by Wharton, MIT and London Business School has proven that laughter relieves stress and boredom, defuses tension and negativity, increases engagement, promotes wellbeing and positivity, inspires creativity, builds relationships, fosters collaboration, improves motivation and morale, aids learning, hones analytic precision and raises productivity. [*Takes breath*] Yeah—so there's all of that.

Many companies are perfectly comfortable using humour in their marketing, advertising and communication with customers and clients. Which is telling, isn't it? There's obviously a recognition that humour is effective at building relationships, yet these same businesses frequently shy from using humour to connect with their own people.

## Humour surprises and grabs our attention

Because it's often in such short supply at work, using humour strategically can win us attention. It can make everyday communication remarkable and memorable. It can stop us in our tracks and make us look twice.

## Humour builds trust and influence

Studies have shown that leaders who use humour authentically are thought of more highly. Humour makes us more likeable, and with that comes trust. A well-told joke is capable of dragging a begrudging snort out of even the biggest cynic. And for these reasons, humour is a powerful driver of influence.

## Humour builds relationships... and culture

Big call, huh? It shouldn't come as too much of a shock, though. Humour is inherently human, releasing a heady cocktail of pleasurable chemicals every time we're amused. Laughter has also been proven to be important in building rapport. Considering strong relationships are fundamental to effective collaboration, as well as forming the foundation for any strong culture, there's a compelling case for chasing a chuckle.

## The universal appeal of being amusing

Humour is a full-brain workout: limbic system, cerebral cortex, occipital lobe, amygdala and hippocampus all pumped up. These are the areas associated with linguistics, meaning, emotional responses, motivation and behaviour.

Our physiological response to humour is laughter. It stimulates the production of serotonin, which makes us happy, and triggers the production of endorphins, which gives us a natural high. This is why we want to be amused; it's the reason we like to laugh. Laughter is so potent, it can even briefly override other emotions, including anxiety and fear.

Researchers also believe that laughter serves a social function — essential to building and strengthening relationships. It's no coincidence that humour is frequently used by advertising, marketing and sales. We tend to buy from people or brands we like, and laughter builds that rapport. Attention, likeability, shareability — these are the foundations those industries are built on, and humour ticks all three boxes.

When it comes to what makes us laugh, there are three common theories.

The *incongruity theory* explains humour that surprises us with the unexpected. We anticipate a certain conclusion based on logic or past experience, but an unforeseen twist forces us to experience two incompatible thoughts and emotions simultaneously. For example: *There are two fish in a tank. One turns to the other and says, 'Do you know how to drive this thing?'*

The *superiority theory* involves jokes that make fun of someone's/ something's stupidity, mistakes or misfortune. This type of humour works when we believe ourselves superior. It's a style that's often used by comics, where the hero's foolish nemesis is subjected to ongoing indignities for our depraved amusement.

The *relief theory* explains how humour can relieve tension. This type of humour is often used in movies. A witty one-liner gives temporary relief before suspense is built again.

Some types of humour are universally well received. These include in-jokes, slapstick and any joke relating to the fundamental similarities among all people (read: toilet humour). In contrast, highbrow, irony, sarcasm, puns, wordplay and subtle linguistics can translate badly. And political, religious, racial or cultural stereotypes are always a terrible idea.

> **We tend to buy from people or brands we like, and laughter builds that rapport.**

That isn't to say humour can't be a little spicy.

Marketing and Psychology professor Peter McGraw's *Benign Violation* theory suggests that humour happens when we find something wrong, unsettling or threatening, but simultaneously okay, acceptable or safe. It's the balance of the two contradictory elements that makes a joke amusing *and* appropriate. Slip too far one way, the joke turns offensive. Tilt the other way, it loses its edge.

So what might humour look like when incorporated into communication at work? Gather round the metaphorical campfire and let your old pals tell you a story about Liam and his intrepid Field Sales troop.

## Liam laughs in the face of adversity

Last we spoke of Liam and his Field Guide, he was using mindfulness to keep people safe on the job. Emotions were an important part of Liam's induction experience, but it wasn't his only cleverness.

The Field Guide replaced the typical induction manual (you know the type: heavy on detail and light on impact) with a handbook that people actually wanted to read. Liam wanted an artefact that his Field Sales team carried with them at all times.

The solution was to strip the manual back to the bare essentials, visualising the content, and making it engaging for a diverse workforce where English was often a second language. It incorporated the content into a 12-month mindfulness journal, including plenty of planning space and interesting information to keep people turning the pages.

The concept for the Field Guide riffed on the fact that Field Sales people are generally out on the road, in the wilds (metaphorically) and out in the field (sort-of-literally). A field guide is traditionally an illustrated manual detailing wilderness environments, and in some cases teaching people how to survive in them.

The illustrations used in the guide were firmly tongue-in-cheek—bringing wilderness elements (think: bears) into typical urban retail environments, and depicting the Field Sales team as rugged, woodsy types clad in flannel. The writing was pulled back to basics and written in the straightforward, matter-of-fact tone found in typical field guides. A conversational (often cheeky) edge to the writing made it easy and fun to read.

Liam's Field Guide worked exactly as he'd hoped. Feedback from new recruits expressed how they'd been drawn into reading the manual cover to cover and had learned a lot in the process. As a first step to preparing people for the realities of work and inducting them into Field Sales culture, it couldn't have been a better result. Liam proved that humour doesn't need to be over-the-top or laugh-out-loud. A wry smile can be enough.

## The risky business of being funny

The Field Guide worked because it brought the right type of funny. The scenarios were ridiculous, but they were based on common situations that all Field Sales employees could relate to and laugh about together (remember the incongruity and relief theories). Most importantly, humour made the content interesting. It drew people's attention and compelled them to keep reading. Ultimately, it achieved Liam's objective of improving his Field Sales team's performance out on the job.

Unfortunately, while leaders like Liam are bold enough to bring humour into their work, many workplaces are missing out on the potential benefits. A recent study of Gallup data found that we laugh significantly less on weekdays than we do on weekends. Research by Eric Tsytsylin describes working adults as in the midst of a laughter drought. Babies laugh on average around 400 times a day. Over 35, and we're lucky to crack 15. Apparently, work has become serious business.

With all the benefits of humour, why is it still in such short supply in so many organisations?

One word: *risk*.

The hurdle to using humour effectively is that it can be subjective, contextual and culturally specific. If we can't relate to the joke for any one of these reasons, we won't find it funny. Worse, if we do relate to the joke, but perceive it's in poor taste or at our expense, we'll take offence. This makes it challenging to choose the right type of humour to appeal to everyone, especially in a large-scale or global roll-out.

**The hurdle to using humour effectively is that it can be subjective, contextual and culturally specific.** Of all the factors that influence what we find amusing, culture is obviously important, but age also makes a significant difference.

When we're an infant or toddler, we're in a period of discovery. At this age, our world is an endless source of ridiculous, surprising and hilarious situations. This is one of the reasons youngsters find bodily functions so funny.

By the time we reach our teens, we're at our most awkward and insecure. We're amused by sex, food, authority figures and any subject considered taboo by adults. We tend to use humour for protection and to demonstrate superiority.

As we get older, though, our sense of humour changes. Don't get me wrong, we're every bit as amused by a fart, but in general our sense of humour becomes a little more cerebral. We're amused by the typical stresses and embarrassments we experience. Politics, family and job pressures—if we didn't laugh, we'd probably cry. Humour is one of our coping mechanisms (remember: *relief theory*).

With organisations comprising up to five generations, we need to be aware of our differences and similarities to ensure our humour hits the mark.

Finally, while humour can cut through the noise, it's not immune to habituation (explored a few chapters ago). Wheeling out the same joke over and over causes an audience to tune out faster than when Granddad tells the story about the time when he was young and...

Yeah, you get the idea.

# How to speak…
# humour

### Idea #17: Find the right type of funny

There's really just one goal when it comes to humour: make it funny. But how do we ensure our humour lands?

To find the right type of funny, we can:

- Look for the commonalities. The best jokes are the ones everyone relates to, the ones that bring us together. We need to look for the typical stressors and situations that could be turned into something we can all laugh at. This can bring a sense of relief and reduce anxiety around an issue.

- Use different types of humour to appeal to different groups. This might be segmented by age, role or geography. The smaller the group, the easier it is to appeal to everyone with the same type of humour.

- Push it beyond normal—make it utterly ridiculous. Find the most extreme version of a situation or persona. Making it completely unrealistic reduces the risk of the joke being taken too literally or hitting too close to home. Slapstick works well for this reason.

# Caution...

## The complication of complexity

Ever seen a three-year-old engaged by a book on physics (bludgeoning ants with it doesn't count)? Ever observed a frontline worker highly engaged by a policy manual during their lunch break? Ever witnessed a room full of people engaged out of their brains by a 500-slide technical PowerPoint presentation?

Yep, we don't stand a chance at engaging or influencing anyone with complex communication. We'd be flat out just getting their attention.

And here's our challenge. Absolutely anyone can make exciting subject matter thrilling, but the real kicks come from turning the most mind-numbing and complicated content into simple and captivating fare.

Fortunately, there's nothing that can't be made interesting and nothing that can't be made simple; it just comes down to a shift in perspective.

### Complexity isn't the enemy

Picture a Swiss Army knife resplendent with multipurpose, and we challenge you not to think of the word 'prepared'. From the brutality of its form to the savagery of its function, you could go into the wilderness right now, it suggests, with no more than this small piece of plastic and steel, and survive. It's a tool that proudly proclaims preparation for whatever life hurls at you... Unless you tote the Butler's model, which prepares you for very little beyond an impromptu picnic in the park.

Yes, for many of us *preparation* is simply the promise that no pinot remains impenetrable when we need to slake a vicious thirst. But, beyond cleaving cheese and smallgoods, let's appreciate the Swiss Army knife for what it truly is: a ridiculous 87 tools with 141 unique functions somehow squeezed into a rectangle small enough to slip snug into a pocket.

Small enough not to think twice about taking, enough functions to make taking it worthwhile. The Swiss Army knife is the very embodiment of preparation and perfectly encapsulates simplicity: complex function hidden behind a simple interface through clever design.

From iPhones to navigating the Metro, from Google searches to our brains, we constantly underestimate the sheer complexity of things when they're well designed. It's easy to assume that everything that seems simple is simple, because the successful resolution of complexity renders it invisible.

**Fortunately, complexity doesn't need to be confusing. Complexity can certainly be engaging.** Dealing with complexity has escalated in importance as business has become increasingly intricate. It falls on leaders to take complex ideas, messages, processes, policies and strategies, and develop them into more engaging experiences and communication. It's a process that involves diving headlong and intrepid into complexity, searching for sense and simplicity. And that's where it gets really interesting.

By definition, simplicity is the opposite of complexity, but let's harpoon the belief that it's either one or the other. Simplicity shouldn't be seen as merely an exercise in subtraction either. Both notions are far too simplistic.

The world is complex. Humans are complex. Life is complex. Work is complex. We deal with inherent complexity daily. It's naive to think we should—or can—solve complexity just by eliminating details. That isn't simplicity, that's just dumbing it down. Removing detail is robbing the richness that makes things interesting, stripping the features that make them useful.

Heck, simplifying complexity isn't even the issue we should be trying to solve.

No, our objective should be attention, engagement and influence — making a difference. And the real challenge to making things interesting, engaging, enjoyable, influential, inspiring, informative and clear isn't actually complexity...

It's *confusion*.

Fortunately, complexity doesn't need to be confusing. Complexity can certainly be engaging. We just need to make the complicated easy to understand. Make things understandable and they'll seem simple. Make things seem simple, and we remove one of the biggest barriers to engagement.

So how do we do it?

It's really quite simple...

## Simple, not simpler

Before we go further, let's pause and point out an elephant: WE'RE WRITING ABOUT SIMPLICITY HERE, PEOPLE! And with that acknowledgement comes a terrible burden: the possibility of complicating a section about simplicity. Because, if there's one thing we know for certain, it's simplicity ain't simple. It isn't a matter of hacking out the bits that are tough to deal with. It's resolving them so you don't even notice they're there.

A Google search shows a single input box while concealing algorithms that tear through 4.74 billion pages to find and filter results in less time than it takes to blink. Hidden within the unassuming exterior of an iPhone lies the ability to connect with the world. Cameras capture a moment in time with the click of a button. The theory of relativity — as elegant and memorable as $E=mc^2$.

Ernest Hemingway's writing is renowned for its simplicity. Direct and unadorned, reserved use of adjectives — the simplicity of the language means almost anyone can read his stories. Yet what appears simple and effortless is actually built on an intricate system of repetition and symmetry. His prose is stripped of the superfluous, but it remains evocative because of what he *chooses* to include. Each word is so important that changing one could throw it all off-key. It's far from simple, but Hemingway does it so well that we just don't notice.

We're not Google, nor (sadly) are we Hemingway. But we do know about simplicity. And what we know is that it doesn't matter if it's a product, a piece of communication, a service or an experience—the same fundamentals apply. Make things easy to understand, and they'll seem simple. Make things simple, and they become far more likely to be useful.

But enough of the theory, what about the practice? Well, complexity can be simplified through eight considerations.

## Begin with understanding

We begin by understanding the content. Oh yes, so appallingly obvious-sounding, yet with everything a leader needs to get done in a day, this is an easy item to skip—thus skipped frequently.

We have a *general* idea of the information, right? We've been using this content for the past decade so it *must* be okay, right? It just needs a little... *zhuzhing*, right?

Oh so wrong!

If we want to cut through complexity we need to immerse ourselves in the source material and understand it implicitly. No assumptions; no shortcuts; no hiding old cracks behind new wallpaper. If we want to get this right, we need to invest the time up front.

## Follow with context

Once we understand what we've got, we can ask ourselves *why* we're doing whatever it is we're doing.

Why does it exist? Who's it for? What purpose does it serve? What problem does it solve? Where will it be experienced? What are the expectations? So many questions, but all of them (and more) are necessary.

Simplicity and comprehension are both highly contextual. Simplicity in one circumstance may be complexity in another. Someone's simplicity is someone else's complexity. Two physicists might have a thoroughly fascinating discussion about relativity, but you'd best come at us with *Science For Dummies* if you expect even a rudimentary conversation.

This isn't a notion reserved for rocket scientists and neurosurgeons, though; there's complexity in any specialisation. From making great coffee, to manufacturing staples, to ensuring the trains run on time — we should consider what simplicity means to our intended recipient or user.

Revisiting the Swiss Army knife, we see an excellent example of context. In everyday situations, each function is better performed by an implement engineered specifically for that purpose: a regular screwdriver, a proper cheese knife, a decent corkscrew.

Squeezing a toolbox into miniature means making compromises. In the intended context of adventure, however, when weight, size and portability are the key considerations, these compromises are far outweighed by having all the functions at hand.

The simplicity of the Swiss Army knife comes from understanding the context in which it will be used, the ruthless exclusion of the unnecessary and the inclusion of only the most relevant.

This segues very satisfactorily into ...

## Sift for relevance

Once we understand the context, then we can sift for relevance. What's necessary, and what's the simplest way we can say or show the content? What details really matter? What will our intended audience relate to? What helps us solve the problem?

Let's strip it right back to basics. Remove all the bullshit, the buzzwords, the abstract language, the corporate jargon and the redundancies. Let's remove the unnecessary, but — caution! Simplicity shouldn't be mistaken for minimalism. Where simplicity comes from understanding and resolving complexity, minimalism is merely a stylistic treatment. While effective simplicity is invisible, minimalism is often all too obvious—at a cost to comprehension.

Yes, a sure side effect of oversimplification is—quite perversely—confusion. Oh, the wonderful irony in that! Stripping things too far back and removing meaningful information can easily introduce confusion and cognitive load as we struggle to make sense.

Removing text from icons can make a user interface less intuitive and more difficult to navigate. Minimalism in architecture looks beautiful... until someone inhabits it. Life is full of big, beautiful mess, detail and complexity. It's certainly easier to remove detail than address it, but that's not what simplicity is really about.

Quite counterintuitively, simplicity can sometimes be better achieved through addition. Yes, in cheeky contradiction of our inclination to include less, more is often ... more. As well as asking what can be removed, let's also ask what we can add. How might we introduce more richness, meaning, function, purpose and humanness into our work?

**Stripping things too far back and removing meaningful information can easily introduce confusion and cognitive load as we struggle to make sense.** In 2016, the London Underground updated their tube maps and, contrary to the typical minimalist approach used in transport applications, included the number of steps between each station, revealing instances when it would actually be easier to walk to the destination, rather than waiting to cram into another crowded compartment for a very short trip.

This solution demonstrates an understanding of context and relevance, and how the right treatment of complexity can create a better experience. At first glance the design appears more complicated, yet ultimately it makes people's lives simpler.

This transitions us nicely into ...

### Start from scratch

Only now, *finally*, can we start from scratch, and make it again as simply as possible. Even if—*especially* if—it cuts the content in half (which it often will). This is about communicating only what's necessary in as few words as possible.

## Make it for humans

Once we've got the bare bones, then we can flesh it out. Now's the time to add the human.

Because, whether we're delivering a service, developing a product, designing an experience or communicating, our purpose is to connect with people. And speaking human doesn't just help us make things worthy of attention, engaging and influential, it also helps us make them simple.

Empathy helps us establish context and relevance. Curiosity inspires learning. Emotions drive our choices at the most basic level. Storytelling establishes a deeper connection. Conversations help us improve future iterations.

If we were to include this garnish earlier, we'd only risk adding unnecessary confusion without purpose—polishing the proverbial.

And, when it comes to humans, here's another truth...

## Reduce our hefty cognitive burden

Busy and overwhelmed have become our new normal. There's a constant clash and clamour for our attention, and a seemingly infinite number of decisions that need to be made daily.

It's estimated that we make around 35 000 conscious choices every day, each one expending precious mental energy. Make too many decisions in too short a timeframe and our decision making abilities dramatically decrease.

Hooray, free will.

It's no wonder folk will do whatever it takes to shave a few decisions from their day. Steve Jobs was known for his deliberate sartorial monotony, suiting up in a self-imposed uniform of turtleneck, jeans and sneakers. Obama, Zuckerberg and Einstein also championed donning the same duds daily—saving cerebral stamina for decidedly more important issues.

We don't need to start stocking our wardrobes with a week's worth of turtlenecks, but we can do our bit to lighten the cognitive load for others.

There's only so much information we can process, so many decisions we can make, before our gears start grinding. Psychologists refer to this assault on our working memory as *cognitive load*. And when this load becomes too weighty, it dramatically affects our ability to complete tasks.

Psychologists Hick and Hyman discovered that each choice we have to make increases the time it takes us to make a decision. Which isn't ideal if we're trying to help people work efficiently.

To manage cognitive load, psychologists recommend we reduce extraneous load, manage intrinsic load and maximise germane load. Or, in plain English: understand the complexity involved, remove the barriers to understanding it and make the learning methods effective. Oh yes, make it easy, make it simple, and people will be far more likely to act.

So we begin by limiting the choices. This doesn't necessarily mean removing all the options, but we can break them down and deliver them in more manageable blocks. This is one of the reasons filters are frequently used in online shopping, using our preferences to narrow the options and make it more likely we'll purchase something without getting overwhelmed.

Next, we need clear and unambiguous language when comprehension matters most.

We're certainly not advocating dumbing it down. Oversimplifying the intellectual content robs it of the detail that makes it useful. We simply need to reduce the number of possible interpretations.

Let's cull the jargon when communication extends beyond a niche audience. It seeps so insidiously into our language, clouding the message and perpetuating confusion.

Eliminating ambiguity also means avoiding words with multiple meanings. Homonyms, homographs, homophones and syntactic ambiguity all add unnecessary confusion. We're confused just using them in the previous sentence, so let's look at a couple of examples.

'You have a green light' is completely ambiguous without context. 'Tim saw the man with a telescope' could refer to Tim observing a man who had a telescope, or Tim looking through a telescope and seeing a man. Each is a valid interpretation but describes a very different scenario.

We also need to be wary of implicature in our language. This is meaning that's suggested, rather than explicitly expressed. It relies on the listener interpreting our intent based on context, shared knowledge, our relationship, and even the time and place our conversation occurs.

**Or, in plain English: understand the complexity involved, remove the barriers to understanding it and make the learning methods effective.**

We use implicature surprisingly often in social situations. What we leave unsaid can be an intentional or subconscious choice. It can communicate an entirely different message from the actual words we use.

If someone asks us if we can reach the salt, we know they aren't asking if our arm is literally long enough — they're politely asking us to pass it to them. They know that we know what they mean (why is socialising so unnecessarily complicated?).

Interesting sidebar: we often use indirect language to avoid expressing boldness or dominance. It's not really coffee or tea we're offering when we invite someone home at the end of a triumphant first date. Similarly, 'If you could pass the mustard, that would be amazing' doesn't indicate the magnitude of our gratitude for condiments.

Then there's my personal favourite: irony. Oh, the scathing humour we can elicit when our words say one thing but the subtext is exactly the opposite. Used discerningly and cunningly, irony can be extremely effective. Done poorly, though, it can be downright confusing.

Switching from verbal to visual, we can simplify lengthy and complex content using imagery. In 'Visual', we thrilled to our brain's ability to process images around 60 000 times faster than text, and that's one heck of a way to reduce cognitive load. This is one of the reasons important signage is often accompanied by a symbol, why wikiHow uses illustrations, and the only way any of us manage to assemble anything from IKEA.

**Similarly, 'If you could pass the mustard, that would be amazing' doesn't indicate the magnitude of our gratitude for condiments.**

If you're expecting another segue, you'll not be disappointed. We're six for six here friends, and the mention of visual leads us uncannily into our seventh...

### Establish a ruthless order

Without dropping too deep into theory (unnecessary complexity), it's worth knowing that there are principles that influence how we make sense of things visually.

Back in the 1920s, a group of German psychologists discovered that our minds are constantly searching for order and simplicity in even the most seemingly chaotic and complex arrangements. They summarised these findings in a fascinating and delightfully German-sounding theory, Gestalt.

To summarise: we subconsciously group elements that are similar, connected, close, enclosed together, continuing or moving in the same direction, or parallel to each other. Also, our minds have a tendency to complete unfinished objects or patterns. We're agitated by the incomplete (hello, crosswords, jigsaws and connect-the-dots puzzles).

In addition to Gestalt, we can also make it easier to process information through hierarchy. Scale, colour and weight all help convey an order of importance. Newspapers and publications are a fine example, breaking content into weighted headlines, subheadings and body copy to increase comprehension.

Sequence is important too—either prioritising the most important or attention-seizing features, or beginning with the basics and establishing the fundamentals before going deeper.

And so we come to our final tactic, where your old pals have been stubbornly trying to coax a segue for the past 30 minutes. We only need one sentence, but... nothing. So, onwards without transition.

Whatever.

## Remember: recognition over recall

Back into our brains, and our predilection for recognition over recall. More simply: we find it easier to recognise things we've previously experienced rather than recalling specific information from memory.

The simplest systems don't require us to remember specific procedures or processes; they use familiar signals and cues to guide us to the desired outcome.

When we ooze bleary and befuddled from an all-night flight into a foreign country, we generally aren't at our sharpest. Yet no matter how groggy-minded, we still manage to negotiate mazes of generic terminal walkways and travelators with relatively little difficulty. This is a result of effective wayfinding systems, using familiar signs and symbols to simplify the complexity of navigating an unfamiliar environment.

# Words
## The power of using and choosing words wisely

There's something undeniably wonderful — magical, even — about the way well-chosen words can make us feel. Well-crafted writing catches us up and carries us away, to wherever and whenever the writer wants to take us; just as well-delivered speeches wrench the air from our lungs and draw us towards new ideas and ideals.

Unfortunately, when it comes to words at work, most of us can relate to a meeting that goes something like this:

Cue an overenthusiastic young buck or go-getting doe leaping from their chair and bounding across the room. 'We *need* to think outside the box', they declare sagely. 'If we're *really* going to embrace blue-sky thinking, we *need* to reach into the bottom drawer for a competitive advantage.' Another pause to let the significance of that statement sink in. Then, a strong finish. 'I'm sure this is already on everyone's radar. There's lots of moving parts, but with a robust strategy we'll innovate a solution. It's just going to take some heavy lifting ...'

Everyone's nodding. We're nodding. We're all in *alignment*. We're definitely *singing from the same hymn sheet*. We're dying to get back out there and *value-add*. But, quite honestly, we're fairly fucking confused about what we're meant to be value-adding to.

Here's the thing, though ... [*whispers*] No-one else has any idea either.

This is just one example of a business lexicon gone wrong. Jargon-laden meetings, endless-scroll emails padded with waffle, vague instructions. While they're often given little thought as they're pounded out on keyboards or creaking from our voice boxes, the words we hear, read, say and write have a colossal impact.

What could be more important to business than the words we use? They're fundamental to communication, obviously. They allow us to share information with each other. But they also build or undermine relationships. They foster a sense of belonging or a feeling of exclusion. They can inspire, motivate and rally others to action. They can change people's behaviours. They can shift and shape culture.

Let's get words right, lest we start referring to brainstorming sessions as *thought showers*. ☂ 🧖

## Words worthy of attention

In a world and workplace flooded with countless words competing for our attention, the ones that are clear, direct, relevant and surprising are the ones we focus on first. There's no sugar-coating it: this takes effort. But it's effort well spent when it means the difference between our message connecting or missing the mark.

## Words inspire action

Ever noticed how great leaders always seem to know exactly what words will compel people to act? It's not voodoo, though. When we analyse their words, there's a recurrent swing between formal and colloquial; passive and active; relational and rhetorical. The only constant is that their words always ring authentic.

## Words bring people together or tear them apart

What are the words your culture is built on? Is it a culture of inclusiveness—*us* and *we*? Or a culture of individuals—*I* and *me*? Even this tiny distinction can change the dynamics of our teams and the way they work together.

## Active versus passive

What do we want people to *do*? The verbs we use and the way we arrange our words can compel people to act or respond. An important part of making this happen is choosing between *passive* and *active* voice.

*Passive* voice is a wonderful choice when we want communication to be unbiased and objective, which is why it's often used for scientific reports and reputable news reporting. But it tends to produce tepid messaging. The *active* voice is often tighter, less wordy, more direct and easier to understand. It's more likely to translate into action.

How do we know which voice we're using? The simple rule is to ensure our subject is doing the action, rather than the action being done to the subject. 'The cat bit her owner' versus 'the owner was bitten by the cat'. There's more impact when we put the emphasis on the feline.

What does this look like in action?

Well, instead of saying, 'An email will be sent to confirm the details', we could say, 'I will confirm the details by sending an email'. Instead of messaging, 'Instructions will be given to you by the site coordinator', we could send, 'The site coordinator will give you instructions'.

In both of these examples, we're being more direct and assigning responsibility and accountability.

Think about the people you work with every day. Who tends towards the passive voice, and who favours the active voice? Active voice comes across as more direct and authoritative. However, it can be construed as a little brusque when used too frequently. This is why we like to dial up the human.

We could change the previous examples to:

'I'll confirm the deets by shooting you an email.'

'Our site coordinator, Paul, will give you instructions.'

As long as the additions are authentic, appropriate and dovetail with our company's culture—let rip.

## Loaded language

Our choice of words can also influence others' actions by evoking emotions. This devious technique is known as *loaded language* (also: *emotive language* or *high-inference language*).

It's a trick abused regularly by politicians, public figures and brands, who exploit our tendency to act on our initial emotional response without thinking it through. It's a tactic best used for good, and avoided when fairness or neutrality is needed.

Think of words like 'torture' and 'freedom'. These words carry an emotional charge that resonates beyond their literal meaning. They trigger a subconscious value judgement that escalates into an emotion.

Consider the difference between '*invading* Iraq' and '*liberating* Iraq'. Were their wages 'reduced' or 'slashed'? Is a new 4WD a 'cost' or an 'investment in lifestyle'?

What loaded language is used, or can be used, in your workplace?

## Rhetorical versus relational

All workplace communication comprises *rhetorical* and *relational* language.

*Relational* language is exactly what it sounds like: it's used in conversations that forge connections, build trust and credibility, and foster collaboration. It can be as simple as asking someone what they got up to on the weekend or a conversation about sports during a lunch break.

On the other hand, *rhetorical* language is all about influence, persuasion, argumentation and getting others to bend to our point of view. It's frequently used in presentations and meetings, and whenever we're asking someone to do something.

While the origins of rhetoric can be traced all the way back to ancient Greece, the fundamentals still hold true. It incorporates three distinct styles: *agility* (*logos*) employs logic; *authenticity* (*ethos*) appeals to hopes and dreams, ideals, morals, values, and guiding beliefs of a community or culture; and *empathy* (*pathos*) is about care and appeals primarily to our emotions.

Influence isn't only about rhetorical language, though; we need a balance of styles to communicate effectively. It's all too obvious when a leader tilts too far into rhetoric, just as it is when conversations linger too long in the relational.

## Abstract versus concrete

Abstract language is intangible and vague. It references big ideas, concepts, themes and categories. But because it lacks tangibility, it also tends to lack emotional impact.

Conversely, concrete language evokes a visceral visual image. It uses specific words to paint a compelling picture that's rich in detail. 'Imagine' is a particularly powerful word because it encourages us to visualise an outcome.

Effective communication dances between abstract and concrete words, yet business communication—strategy in particular—frequently floats in abstraction.

It's an easy trap to fall into: sweeping, cliché-heavy proclamations like, 'let's focus on the key priorities', or, 'our customers come first'. But what do those statements really mean?

Using generic language assumes everyone shares the same definitions of words like 'loyalty', 'accountability', 'culture', collaboration', 'alignment' and 'results'. Yet business terms and buzzwords rarely make for compelling or influential language.

No, if we want to bring our vision to life, we need to swing our language into the concrete.

Consider a typical organisational value set: Excellence, Integrity, Respect, Teamwork, Safety. All wonderful words, ideals that are well worth aspiring to. But what do they actually look like on a daily basis? Unless we unpack the behaviours and share what they look like throughout the employee lifecycle, they'll no doubt remain words—not values.

Now, look at the values of Ueno Digital: *We're all in this together, Be raw, Figure it out, Nothing here is someone else's problem, Bring the chocolate, Life is short, enjoy it.* While these 'Culture Values™' still need to be unpacked, they paint a more detailed and memorable picture than *empathy, transparency, courage, self-awareness, motivation* and *gratitude*. Not only is this concrete language, but it's decidedly human as well.

## Formal versus colloquial

For several centuries, formal was the default at work, but our appetite for formality today is significantly different. The trend towards human has brought a craving for language abundant with colloquialism and other informalities.

The appropriate level of formality should be determined by context, brand, culture and audience — never by outdated notions of professionalism.

In Australia, for example, there's an odd phenomenon where the more colloquially we speak, the more we're liked. Conversely, the more formally we speak, the less we're trusted. Our national culture bends towards underdogs, battlers and blue collars. Of course, this is different for everyone, depending on where we are in the world, which company we work for and what industry we work in.

Regardless, the one thing that should never be tolerated is *jargon* (hands up if you thought it was going to be swearing?). Jargon is insidious, the very worst of formal speak. At Jaxzyn, we don't have a swear jar, we have a 'jar-gon'. If anyone uses unnecessary terminology, everyone is encouraged to call it out. The word is written on a piece of paper and put into the jar-gon as an act of penitence.

## Familiar and inclusive

People speaking different languages find it tougher to communicate with each other, but comprehension doesn't only apply to speakers of different nationalities.

**This is where we need empathy to look beyond what seems natural to us and to use language that's familiar to the people we want to connect with.** A neurosurgeon and a builder both have their own languages. A developer at Atlassian speaks a different language from an executive at Nestlé. A safety leader speaks a slightly different language from someone working in sales. And while there are certainly commonalities, language can easily become a barrier to comprehension and influence.

Simply: it's easier to understand language we use regularly.

The challenge is that language varies across age groups, cultural backgrounds, socioeconomic backgrounds and roles. This is where we need empathy to look beyond what seems natural to us and to use language that's familiar to the people we want to connect with.

Beyond comprehension, familiar language also fosters inclusion. Unfamiliar language emphasises our differences rather than our similarities. If we're working towards a sense of community, commonality and shared purpose, we should also be working towards a common language that feels familiar to everyone.

So how do we keep it familiar and inclusive?

Well, if our people are prolific jargon users, perhaps we can include a jargon cheat sheet in our induction kits.

Setting context before diving into content also goes a long way to ensuring everyone feels included. This might mean starting meetings by framing where we've come from and where we're at.

Finally, let's say things simply. If Stephen Hawking could explain time travel in a way that most of us can understand, there really shouldn't be much that can't be said in a way that's universally understood. We just need to invest a bit more effort.

## Inclusion versus exclusion

Our choice of pronoun also defines our relationships with others. Changing a single word can bring us together or set us apart.

'We' and 'us' is inclusive, while 'you' and 'I' is exclusive. Is it *me* and *you*, or *us* together?

Let's consider these in a work context.

We often hear: 'The CEO sent an email to all employees'. But what about: 'Our CEO sent us all an email'. Simply using 'our' and 'us' brings everyone together facing the same challenges. It fosters a sense of inclusion and unity.

It's no accident which particular pronouns are used most frequently in this book.

# How to speak …
# words

### Idea #18: Words matter

There's power in words, friends. We can change the way we're perceived and understood, and how others feel, simply by choosing our words carefully.

Communication isn't limited to painstakingly prepared meetings and presentations, though. We're judged on every single interaction, the daily conversations and banter—heck, even when we say nothing it can be interpreted as something.

So to use words well, we can:

- Use the active voice. Make the subject *do* something.

- Use loaded language—but with caution. Words that carry an emotional charge can be incredibly powerful at rallying people to act. Any time we light a fire, though, there's the potential we'll get burned.

- Use a balance of relational and rhetorical language. We need to foster relationships, but there are also times when we need people to see things from our perspective.

- Translate abstract visions, strategies and concepts into concrete language. Let's go beyond vague leadership clichés like 'integrity' and 'excellence', and bland business tropes like 'alignment' and 'value'. Let's paint a more detailed and evocative picture.

- Be wary of formality. There's always a matter of what's appropriate, but old notions of professionalism can be detrimental to connection.

- Use language that feels familiar to the people we're communicating with. This fosters inclusion and comprehension.

- Use 'we' and 'us' to demonstrate unity. We're in this together.

- Use words that come naturally. Let's push past the generic corporate lexicon and impersonal tone, and show some personality. Nothing is as unsettling or obvious as words that don't ring true.

- Kill unnecessary jargon when it risks alienating people or causing confusion.

# Names
## The undeniable sweetness of a well-chosen name

It's somewhat ironic that Shakespeare, a man whose reputation is tied to words, penned the line 'a rose by any other name would smell as sweet'. In our old pal Willy's play *Romeo and Juliet*, Juliet indulges in a good old-fashioned soliloquy to convince herself that it doesn't matter that Romeo has the surname 'Montague'. She insists his name makes no difference, even if it is the name of her family's arch-enemy.

Almost everyone knows how things worked out for those two loved-up optimists, but the real tragedy here is that this line has been parroted for the better part of 400 years whenever someone wants to belittle the importance of a name.

*'A rose by any other name would smell as sweet...'*

No! The play's ending alone negates the argument, but research also proves Juliet was wrong. Names *do* matter. They influence the way we think about and remember things. They define and shape relationships.

Over the past 15 years we've helped name numerous programs, initiatives and events. One we recall particularly easily was renaming the very literal, and decidedly unmemorable, *Systems Meeting*. The event brought hundreds of leaders from around the globe to plan for the next five years. This came at a considerable cost, with high expectations for a return on investment.

Such names are all too familiar. *Drivers Manual*, *Leadership Summit*, *Culture Change Program*—these generic titles could belong to any business, and give us little idea of how they might be different, interesting or in any way relevant. In the case of the *Systems Meeting*, the name in no way embodied what the four-day innovation, strategy and planning event could achieve. It sounded much like any other technical meeting held on a weekly basis.

### Names differentiate and help us remember

A well-chosen name elevates an idea and differentiates it from everything that's come before. It makes it unique to our organisation or department, and far more likely to stick in our mind.

### Names influence the way we think

A name can set expectations and convey personality. It can communicate important information about a program, initiative or event before we experience it. This makes naming a powerful opportunity for cognitive framing.

### Names set the tone for our relationships

It's not just about what we call our programs, initiatives and events. What we call other people sets the tone for our relationships. Do we refer to each other by title, family name, given name or nickname?* Do we even know each other's names? Do our role descriptions amplify hierarchy or flatten it? When we're looking to shift culture, how we refer to one another is an important consideration.

### What's in a name?

We promised you proof that names make a difference.

In an adorably academic 'screw you' to Shakespeare, Jelena Djordjevic and pals at McGill University and the Montreal Neurological Institute conducted a study called 'A Rose by Any

---

* At Jaxzyn, we sure do love nicknames. Old Mate, T-Bone, J-Rad, KB, B, Samwise and Nads are just a few.

Other Name: Would It Smell as Sweet?' to find out if the way a scent is named influences how people perceive it.

Turns out, it does. Subjects were served a buffet of 15 scents, from foul to neutral to nice. Each smell was presented with names that were positive ('carrot juice'), neutral (a two-digit number) or negative ('mouldy vegetables'). Perversely, no matter how good or gross the smell, people rated it as more pleasant when it was presented with a positive name, and less pleasant when presented with a negative name. This wasn't a subjective rating, either—it was physiological. When the smell had a positive name, subjects sniffed more, and their skin conductance and heart rate showed greater arousal.

Speaking of smelly things: *children*. Researchers Harari and McDavid found that the names we give our progeny can affect their academic results. The experiment provided a group of teachers with essays to grade. Nothing unusual there, except that the teachers weren't aware that the names on the essays were fake. In a very unfortunate finding for anyone saddled with an uncomely moniker, students with unpopular or unattractive names ('Mildred' or 'Reginald') received significantly lower grades than the kids with attractive or popular names ('Jennifer' or 'Dougal').

Perhaps even more importantly for our offspring's self-esteem, MIT researcher Amy Perfors found that our name can influence how attractive others find us. Perfors posted photos of 24 of her friends at hotornot.com, a site where people are rated on their looks. She compounded this cruelty by posting each photo twice, using two different names. Surprisingly, the same photo received different ratings depending on the name used.

For females, it seems we find full, round-sounding names ('Laura' or 'Sally') more attractive than names with smaller, sharper vowel sounds. For males, names with vowel sounds made at the front of the mouth ('Evan' or 'Ivan') make a man seem more handsome.

The moral of this story is to avoid friendships with psychologists, but also to save yourself hours on the porch with a shotgun during your child's adolescence by bestowing on her a hideous name.

## The pros and cons of putting things in categories

Studies also show we're more likely to remember something when we know its name.

In an experiment veering into the paranormal, psychologist Gary Lupyan showed subjects a series of images of aliens and asked them to guess whether they were friendly or hostile. After each response, they were told if they were right or wrong, helping them learn the subtly distinct features that indicated each alien's intentions.

But here's the twist: before the experiment, a quarter of the group were told that the friendly aliens were known as Leebish and the hostile ones were Grecious; another quarter were told the opposite; and for the remaining half the aliens remained nameless. The results revealed that the half who were told the aliens had names learned to categorise the aliens faster, reaching 80 per cent accuracy in less than half the time taken by the other group.

How we categorise things also influences the way in which we remember them.

In an experiment with much more mundane subject matter, a lucky bunch of participants viewed furniture taken from an IKEA catalogue. In half the questions they were asked to label the object ('chair', 'bed', 'lamp', etc.); the rest of the time they simply had to say whether they liked it or not. Interestingly, in the instances when people labelled the product, they found it more difficult to remember specific details about it later. The act of categorising tends to make things more similar and generic in our minds.

As exciting as extraterrestrials and Swedish furniture are, what do these findings mean for us?

Well, they show how important naming is in learning applications. If we can ensure people remember a name—be it a system, process, program or hazard—they'll find it easier to recall details and facts about it later.

At the same time, we also need to be wary of how things are categorised, especially if we want people to remember specific details. This is particularly relevant when the characteristics are different from what's normally found in that category, or when the category carries negative associations.

Using the word 'program' instantly positions it with a whole set of existing beliefs and assumptions. Which is fine, unless we want people to think about it differently. Perhaps it's better categorised as an 'experience' or 'initiative' — these categories have different connotations.

Using the word 'program' instantly positions it with a whole set of existing beliefs and assumptions.

Even better, if we want people to think about it entirely differently, let's give it a unique and memorable name.

## John and the not boring safe design course

Signing up to an online safe design course isn't often a cause for celebration. Who's spent sleepless nights anticipating learning about the hierarchy of control? And while safe design is an incredibly important topic for architects, engineers and other designers, the content is typically dense, technical and delivered in a passive learning style. Basically: read a whole bunch of stuff and remember it.

John, the founder of a leading safe design company, wanted to develop an online course that designers actually enjoyed. He wanted to combine contemporary learning methodology with the latest technology, and throw in a healthy helping of human. He wanted it to be informative, but also engaging. And because the course would be accredited, it needed to consider and incorporate legislation and policy.

Halfway through developing the course, John started considering what to call it. He needed a name that would accurately convey the experience, a name that encapsulated the human approach to technical content but didn't set unrealistic expectations. At the end of the day it was still a course about safe design, not a holiday at an idyllic locale. Enthusiasm needed to be tempered by realism.

And there it was. With that insight, *The Not Boring Safe Design Course* was born. A name that offers the promise of valuable technical content delivered in an engaging way: a series of short videos packed full of self-deprecating humour, case studies and practical content. An experience that, while probably not fun, certainly isn't boring.

## Change the name, change the perspective

Names and categories are closely connected. Often the name we assign something is also a category, and this is where things get really interesting.

Has calling a department and industry 'Human Resources', implying people are 'resources' and 'assets', perpetuated a point of view that celebrates the pursuit of profit at the expense of people? Have these names influenced the way people have been treated at work, and the way they approach their work as a result?

It sure seems likely, especially as more organisations shift from 'Human Resources' to 'People and Culture' and 'Employee Experience' terminology. While a simple name change might not seem like much, it certainly parallels the trend towards a more human workplace, where people are treated as more than something to be used and expended.

Do we refer to 'resources', 'assets' or 'staff', or do we say 'employees'? Even better, why not use 'our people'? Similarly, are we referring to our customers with generic titles like 'the client', or are we using their names?

Call someone by a name often enough, and not only will we see them that way, but they'll likely begin to see themselves that way too—and act the part. The names and categories we use can actually influence people's perspective and behaviours.

Airbnb uses 'host' to refer to the people offering their properties for rent. There are many options they could have used, but this particular word carries a welcoming tone. Others, like 'landlord', would have conveyed a very different feeling.

**Do we refer to 'resources', 'assets' or 'staff', or do we say 'employees'? Even better, why not use 'our people'?**

Subway calls their people 'artists'—which is a relative term, we guess. Is it simply for the customer's benefit? Or does it also subliminally encourage Subway's people to take pride in a well-crafted sandwich? Perhaps a simple name has the potential to turn a bored teen working in fast food into a ranch-sauce-toting artist attacking foot-longs with the inspired abandon of Jackson Pollock.

## A representation of relationships

Within any culture, language and categorisation play an important social role in constructing group identity and hierarchy.

*Deixis* refers to the way certain words refer to objects, people and places in relation to their position in time and space. This concept is also used to signal social distance between people.

In English, we use given names when we're on familiar terms, and titles like 'sir', 'Mrs', 'Doctor' or 'Your Honour' when we're less familiar, to show respect. Other languages use more complex conventions, with variations depending on gender, age or social class.

In East Asia, different words are used depending on whether the speaker is talking to someone of higher or lower social status. In Australia, the Indigenous language Dyirbal requires a married man to use a specific set of words when speaking in the presence of his mother-in-law.

What deixis exists within our work culture? Do we address each other formally by title or informally by given name? Does our language amplify hierarchy or flatten it? These are important cultural considerations when determining the relationships we want to establish.

# How to speak...
# names

### Idea #19: Name thoughtfully, categorise carefully

Names and categories can seem trivial, yet they play an important role in perception and recall. They convey meaning additional to the message we're intentionally sending.

To name thoughtfully and categorise carefully, we can:

- Consider how we refer to our people. 'Assets', 'resources', 'staff', 'employees', 'people', 'legends', 'pals', 'team'—these all send a clear message about how we see them.

- Consider the names we give our departments, programs, initiatives and clients. These influence the way people think about them.

- Ensure people know the name of important processes, systems, people, hazards, machinery, programs and initiatives. Knowing the name helps us recall the details. This makes naming an important component of learning applications.

- Stay wary of categories—the way we group things together. Categories aid recall, but at the expense of detail. They also carry associations and stigmas that are difficult to break.

- Consider the names and categories we use to label each other. In most Western cultures, using formal titles and full names in communication amplifies organisational hierarchy; using given names flattens it.

TION SURPRISE! HUMOUR VISUAL D
TY HABITUATION FEELS NARRATIVE
CRITY COMPLEXITY CONFUSION EN
ENCE DELIVERY  WORDS NAMING C
RRATIVE LANGUAGE CULTURE ANTIC
GAGEMENT MEDIOCRITY DELIVERY
VE HUMAN ATTENTION INFLUENCE
NGAGEMENT CURIOSITY ANTICIPAT
TION SURPRISE! HUMOUR VISUAL D
TY HABITUATION FEELS NARRATI
CRITY COMPLEXITY CONFUSION EN
NCE DELIVERY  NAMING C
RRATIVE LANGUAGE CULTURE ANTI
GAGEMENT MEDIOCRITY DELIVERY
VE HUMAN ATTENTION INFLUENCE
NGAGEMENT CURIOSITY ANTICIPATI
TION SURPRISE! HUMOUR VISUAL DI
TY HABITUATION FEELS NARRATIVE
CRITY COMPLEXITY CONFUSION ENC
NCE DELIVERY  WORDS NAMING C

# Language
## The power of language
## to shift perception

Whether you believe humans came from ape, idyllic garden or spaceship, it's generally accepted that language evolved (or existed) to facilitate cooperation.

The common scientific theory is that early man-beasts expanded their primate communication systems to work together better. But for those who believe in more spiritual origins, the biblical tale of the Tower of Babel describes how God scattered people with different languages to prevent them working together. Same same.

Language allows us to share knowledge, ideas and stories within our group. Just as importantly, though, it plays a role in protecting that knowledge from outsiders. Oh yes, no matter how cosmopolitan our outlook, our tribal instincts still run deep.

In this way, language has always identified us as belonging to a particular culture, to the exclusion of everyone else. Even when we speak the same language, our accents and dialects reveal our affiliation to various subcultures: nationality, religion, social class, club, gang, team, pastime, political persuasion, trade, profession, employer. It's not uncommon for us to change dialects depending on the cultural setting.

Let's pause a moment here, and look at the word 'culture'. It's a term that's banged on about plenty in the business world, a vague-ish word used to describe a fuzzy set of shared attitudes, beliefs, rituals, conventions, norms, assumptions and values. These all influence our behaviour, how we interpret other people's behaviour and, as a result, the way we interact.

Language is essential in expressing these elements. It encodes the schemas, categories and metaphors that help us make sense of the world. And for this reason, language and culture are woven together, inseparable, each influencing the other.

Many of the business blunders and public gaffes we hear in the news can be traced back to language.

Enron's excesses were no surprise when we consider the typical language used by traders: 'we're an aggressive culture' and 'money is the only thing that motivates'. It wasn't a case of a few folk who went rogue; their shared language sent strong cultural cues about what was considered appropriate behaviour.

More recently, Uber has been beset by accusations of creating a competitive culture in which a blind eye is turned towards the misbehaviour of high achievers. Maybe Uber shouldn't 'always be hustlin'? Perhaps Nike continues to lead their market, with far fewer allegations, because they 'simplify and go' and 'evolve immediately'? These maxims naturally filter through every strategic decision and crucial conversation.

Next opportunity, press an ear to your door or raise your snout above the cubicle divider (so meerkat!), and listen to the language being used in your workplace right now. Filter out the conversations about the previous eve's karaoke debauch or Netflix spoilers, and listen to the way people are talking about business. This is the shared language of your organisation. A language that didn't come straight from a manual or rule book—it evolved naturally.

## Language focuses attention and improves performance

Language can direct our focus and improve performance in certain areas. It shapes what we pay attention to, the things we think about. Are we directing focus towards quality, service or innovation? Is safety woven through our language, keeping it front of mind? Does our language celebrate the collective to improve collaboration?

## Language influences behaviour

Words set expectations and cultural permissions, which are adopted as behaviours. Is our language one of aggression and competition ('take no prisoners!'), or is it inclusive and caring ('our people come first!')? The simplest words seep insidiously into our culture, changing the way people think and act, changing our customers' and employees' experiences.

## Language shapes culture

Above all, our language should foster a shared sense of identity, inclusion, purpose and belonging. It shouldn't amplify our differences, but it should allow for different dialects. The front line will never express things the same way as the exec. Legal will always have jargon that's indecipherable and irrelevant to other departments. There's no single way of saying things that works for everyone.

The challenge is building a shared language based on cultural values, while remaining sensitive to our differences. Because if our language is siloed between departments and teams, it's likely our culture will be fragmented too.

# Watch your language

The language inside our organisations is wrought from the stories and narratives; the values, vision and mission; the branding; the technical terms; the industry and role-specific jargon and acronyms. It flows through conversations, meetings, messaging, emails and memos. It's found in policies, manuals, contracts, our website and the intranet. All these elements (and more) melt together to produce a language that's unique to us.

We all play a role in guiding this shared language. 'Guiding', because we can't completely control it; it's shaped by everyone who belongs to the culture. It needs to flow naturally through daily conversation. People have to *want* to use it. And they need to *mean* what they're saying.

The best we can do is set the tone that echoes through the halls, offices, factories and workplaces. The mantras and maxims, the catch-cries and cultural metaphors, the stories—all filtered into everyday lexicon—are woven into the cultural tapestry. They live beyond brand guides and cultural strategies; they should be as obvious in daily conversations as they are in external press releases and corporate communication.

This language shapes our perspective. It determines our performance. The question isn't 'why does language matter?', but 'why isn't our language treated like it matters more?' And, 'how might we shape the language used in our organisation to drive better results?'

## Anne refreshes the language

Culture change is a monumental undertaking for any organisation. All levels, departments and stakeholders need to get on board. It's tough enough working out where to begin, let alone which of the countless approaches is best suited to our particular needs.

As Head of People and Culture, Anne was responsible for leading her company through a culture change agenda made more challenging by an industry in a state of flux. She had the pivotal role of ensuring their workforce was prepared to meet the needs of tomorrow's customer. No biggie.

Anne went about things a little differently. She began by considering the way their language was shaping their culture. Was it future-focused, all about bold moves and taking chances? Or was it passive, timid, stuck in the past and relying on their reputation? To be ready to face an uncertain future, Anne knew their language needed to be refreshed.

So she organised a series of events, and invited a hundred influencers within the business to reimagine their culture. She also invited a well-known Australian Rules footballer to talk about his experience in fostering a strong team culture. He shared how language, particularly rally cries, unites people with a common sense of purpose, encapsulating a set of beliefs and behaviours.

Following the talk, the group was guided through several activities to begin uncovering and shaping their shared language, starting with a rally cry. These would become the foundations of Anne's cultural strategy over the years to come.

## The circularity of language, thought and culture

Without burying ourselves up to our Aristotles in centuries of philosophical debate, let's just say there have been plenty of opinions about the way language and thought interact. Is thought a form of internal language encoded into our mind? Or is thought independent of language? Chicken, egg; egg, chicken.

It took until the early 1990s and advancements in neuroimaging for a grudging consensus to be reached about the relationship between thought and language. The conclusion? We don't need to know the words for specific concepts in order to think about them. We can imagine the sound of a symphony, the shape of dragon fruit or the smell of freshly mown grass without the vocabulary to describe them.

**The question isn't 'why does language matter?', but 'why isn't our language treated like it matters more?'**

Relatively straightforward, right? However, feeding folk brain-first into the muzzles of fMRI machines also discovered something far more fascinating: subtle but definite differences in the thought patterns of people speaking different languages.

The notion of *linguistic influence*— the idea that language plays a role in guiding thought and perspective — has been proven by linguists, neuroscientists, philosophers and psychologists. Our words can improve comprehension, recall and performance. Our cultural metaphors influence the way we think about certain concepts. The way our language divides broad concepts into specific categories affects the way we think about them. And by focusing our attention, language can improve our performance in certain areas.

In this way, language, thought and culture are all entwined, each influencing the other and, in turn, the way we see the world. These four elements—language, thought, culture and worldview—are connected circularly, a notion that meshes perfectly with the philosophy of linguistic influence.

To summarise, language encodes and regulates:

- what words we use
- what cultural metaphors we use
- how we categorise and split things up
- what we subconsciously focus our attention on.

This impacts:

- how we remember things, events and people
- how we perceive and experience the world
- how we think, and the way we solve problems.

Which are all pretty darn integral to performance, behaviour and culture at work.

So let's dive right in and explore these ideas further. We're going deep now, chums. And truthfully, the next section has the potential to toast your crumpet crispy.

## Words

To state the obvious, the most discernible differences between languages are the words. Obvious doesn't mean inconsequential, though. We've already identified the importance of words; now let's explore how different languages can give the speaker an inherent advantage.

To begin, take a look at these numbers: 5, 8, 3, 9, 2, 7, 4. Read them once, look away for 20 seconds, then repeat them from memory.

How'd you go?

If you failed, don't feel bad. As an English speaker, you had around a 50 per cent chance of remembering the sequence. Ahh, but if you were Chinese, reading those numbers in Mandarin, you likely would have remembered it perfectly.

Why? Well, it's due to a combination of language and memory. We store short-term information in a memory loop with a duration of about two seconds. Whatever we can say or read within those two seconds, we find easier to recall.

Fortunately for Mandarin speakers, their words for numbers are remarkably short. Compare the English word 'seven' and the Mandarin word *qi*. Now, imagine the time difference over seven numbers.

Yes, while English speakers conduct a dexterous oral exercise to get through the sequence, Mandarin speakers can cram all seven numbers into the two-second memory loop, making it more likely they'll remember them.

Now consider the consequences when it comes to learning maths.

Four-year-old Chinese children can generally count up to 40. In comparison, American kids of the same age can count to only 15. They don't make it to 40 for another year, putting them a full year behind their Chinese pals at the most rudimentary mathematical skill.

The Mandarin numbering system also makes more sense than in English, because the language is more logical. In English, we count '11, 12, 13'. In Mandarin, it's '10–1, 10–2, 10–3'. It's a logical system that doesn't require learning completely new words.

Mandarin is also more logical for basic functions like fractions. While English speakers wrap their brain around the concept of 'four-ninths', in Mandarin it's literally explained: 'out of nine parts, take four'.

It's interesting to consider the stereotype of Asian kids dominating at maths, compared with a distinct lack of enthusiasm in English-speaking countries. Perhaps it should come as little surprise that by the time they reach high school, American students rank around thirtieth out of 65 nations, while Chinese and Korean students take the top spots.

Is it all just a coincidence? Cognitive scientist Karen Fuson doesn't think so. She proposes that American kids' disenchantment with maths comes from the clumsy and complicated language system. Chinese children may not necessarily be more intelligent; they simply have an inherent language advantage.

When things are easy, we fight them less, which makes us enjoy them more, which makes us perform better, which leads us right back to enjoying them more. Around and around it goes. It also leads to the logical conclusion that if you want your progeny to dominate at maths, you'd best start teaching them Mandarin.

Then again, there's always someone worse off. The language of the Pirahã tribe in Brazil doesn't have numbers; they simply use 'few' and 'many'. Unsurprisingly, studies show they find it difficult to keep track of exact quantities when dealing with large amounts.

This leads us to some fascinating considerations.

If words can improve our proficiency at maths, how might the words we use at work affect performance? Are our acronyms and jargon increasing the speed and efficiency of our communication, or are they merely causing confusion? Are we contributing to a clumsy and complicated language system? If so, should we purge the specialised language? Or could we foster a strong sense of belonging by ensuring everyone in our organisation understands words that are indecipherable to anyone outside our company culture?

Such possibilities quicken the pulse.

## Metaphors

Linguist George Lakoff suggests our proclivity for metaphors (an average of six per minute) often provides an insight into our cultural values and the way we see the world.

English speakers liken time to money, making it a precious commodity that can be saved, spent, squandered or invested. It can be measured in a wide range of increments: millennia, centuries, decades, years, months, fortnights, weeks, days, hours, minutes, seconds—an indication of an obsession with how much time we invest in various pursuits.

Other languages use different metaphors for time: size, length, even a single, continuous cycle. The Native American Hopi don't refer to today as a new day, it's simply yesterday returning. This notion leads to a very different perspective of time.

English speakers describe duration in terms of length: 'a short talk' or 'it didn't take long'. Greek and Spanish speakers refer to duration in amounts: 'big' or 'much'. It may not seem like a big deal, but these metaphors influence our ability to estimate time.

**Our proclivity for metaphors often provides an insight into our cultural values and the way we see the world.**

Psychologist Daniel Casasanto and cognitive scientist Lera Boroditsky assembled a group of English and Greek speakers, and showed them shapes and objects on a screen for various durations. The English speakers were more easily confused by length: the longer a line was, the longer they thought it stayed on the screen. The Greek speakers were more often confused by amount: they guessed that fuller containers remained on screen longer than emptier ones.

However, the real thrills came from teaching English speakers to speak about time using metaphors from other languages. They were encouraged to describe duration using size, like a Greek speaker, and vertical metaphors to describe the order of an event, like a Mandarin speaker. Changing the metaphor actually changed their thinking to resemble that of a native speaker of Greek or Mandarin.

This wasn't a freak occurrence either. Numerous studies have found that bilinguals change their colour perception, representation of time, emotional expression and other cognitive functions depending on the language they're using.

Let's return to the metaphors we use for time, and think about the potential impact on our work.

For a business that relies on producing a product as quickly and efficiently as possible, a metaphor likening time to money serves them extremely well. However, it may not be as helpful for a company attempting to prioritise quality, safety or service. In these instances, the metaphor subtly undermines these aspirations. When our focus shifts from efficiency to quality, time is no longer a cost, it's a necessary investment.

We wonder, how many business beliefs and assumptions actually come from leadership and company policy, and how many are simply a result of our language? When metaphors aren't serving us, changing them can be an important part of shifting people's perspectives.

## Categories

We explore the idea of categories briefly in 'Names', but different languages also dictate the way we chop up reality. Language determines the groups and categories we use, and how we label them.

Part of learning a language is understanding which things are seen as similar and which are treated differently. While some categories are incontrovertibly defined by science, cultural values dictate how we divide others.

**Language determines the groups and categories we use, and how we label them.** For example, there are—to use the crude vernacular—a shitload of colours smeared across a continuous spectrum. The problem with identifying specific colours is that language isn't continuous. We need to slice up the colour gradient arbitrarily, which each language does differently.

Obviously, it's impossible to give every unique colour a name, though paint brands make a heroic effort. Is that Iceberg White or Polar Bear White? If you can actually tell the difference, there's a legitimate reason for that. Studies show that our brains exaggerate the distinctions between colours and better identify individual colours when they have unique names.

English speakers find it easier to distinguish between blue and green than speakers of languages where blue and green are defined as one colour. However, we find it harder to identify shades of blue than Russian speakers, who have unique words for light blue (*goluboy*) and dark blue (*siniy*).

Gendered languages categorise objects as either male or female. For an English speaker this seems strange, but to a native speaker of a gendered language they're completely natural. Here's the kicker, though: speaking a gendered language can actually help us learn our own gender earlier. Hebrew is a gendered language, while Finnish is not. A study found that kids who speak Hebrew are often aware of their own sex a whole year earlier than their Finnish peers. True story.

The Japanese categorise people as *nihonjin* (Japanese person) and *gaikokujin* or *gaijin* (foreign person). To a Japanese speaker, you're either Japanese or you're not. This may seem slightly offensive, until you consider that it was only relatively recently that Japan opened its borders to outsiders.

Today, Japan remains far less multicultural than other countries, with Japanese making up 98 per cent of the population. In this cultural context, it makes sense that their language categorises people this way. It's rarely considered offensive, though categorising people by race in other cultures most certainly would be. The way language forces us to categorise people provides an interesting insight into the cultural perspective on diversity.

The way we categorise time can influence how likely we are to save money or to smoke.

English is a futured (or strong-future) language, which means that we distinguish clearly between past, present and future. We don't really have a choice in our phrasing: 'the weather *was* foul', 'the weather *is* foul' or 'the weather *will be* foul'.

Languages like Mandarin, German and Japanese are futureless (or weak-future); the same wording can be used to describe an event yesterday, today or tomorrow. Instead of verbs, these languages rely on context to establish the timing of an event.

Why does this matter? Well, behavioural economist Keith Chen believes that the reluctance of Americans to stuff cash into savings accounts, compared with renowned savers like the Chinese, is due to the way language categorises time differently.

To prove his hypothesis, he conducted a study with all the rigour you'd expect from an economist, drawing on vast stores of data to uncover considerable differences between the behaviours of futured and futureless language speakers.

He discovered that futureless language speakers were 30 per cent more likely to save money in any given year, and saved an additional 45 per cent compared with futured language speakers, regardless of which country they lived in.

Chen's findings went well past money, though. Speakers of futureless languages are 20 to 24 per cent less likely to smoke, 13 to 17 per cent less likely to be obese, and 21 per cent more likely to use condoms. Very responsible, but why, exactly?

Well, Chen believes that futured languages make speaking about the future feel further removed and less relevant to us than the present. Why sacrifice certain satisfaction today in favour of something that may or may not happen tomorrow? In contrast, the lack of linguistic distinction between present and future in futureless languages forces the speaker to see them as similar. So next time you pass wads of cash to a cashier instead of stuffing them under your mattress, blame the English language.

**So next time you pass wads of cash to a cashier instead of stuffing them under your mattress, blame the English language.**

In our workplaces, we use categories all the time without giving them much thought. We slice our organisations up in all manner of ways; categorise departments, functions, roles and positions. We delineate friends, colleagues, teammates, bosses, clients and contractors. We even categorise work as 'work' and everything else as 'life'.

But what if we didn't? Or what if it was different? What could work look like with different categories, fewer categories or no categories at all? Perhaps it's time to rethink the way we hole our pigeons. How might our culture change if we rethought the categories that exist inside our organisations?

### Focus

Language may not restrict thought, but it certainly influences what we're obliged to think about. It directs our attention towards specific details. It forces us to include certain information when we communicate.

These obligations are influenced by a combination of cultural values and the language system, particularly the rules that govern comprehension. And because we learn language during our formative years, these considerations become second nature by the time we're adults. We include them in communication subconsciously.

This means that learning a language also requires learning to see the world through a slightly different lens—focusing on different details. These adjustments are enough to shift our perspective, and even the way we think.

English makes us use a tense when we're talking about the timing of an event. Past, present or future—our language leaves no room for ambiguity. French or German forces us to specify the gender of everyone and everything. The simplest message can be open to different assumptions and interpretations depending on the language used.

In English, we use egocentric coordinates like 'left', 'right', 'in front' or 'behind', relative to our position and orientation. Yes, whenever we give directions, the entire world revolves around us. This is far from universal, though. About a third of the world's languages use fixed/cardinal geographic directions. Folk in Polynesia, Mexico, Namibia and Indonesia would use 'north', 'south', 'east' or 'west' instead, these directions remaining constant regardless of which way the speaker is facing.

The difference in navigation systems may seem like semantics, but it encodes a fundamentally different way of seeing the world.

Lera Boroditsky spent time in the remote Indigenous community of Pormpuraaw in Australia, and discovered the way people use directions has some very interesting side effects.

Around one in ten words in a typical conversation is 'north', 'south', 'east', or 'west', often accompanied by appropriate gestures. This means to speak the language properly, you don't just need to know the words, you also need to know the cardinal directions.

If someone greets you, they'd likely ask, 'where are you going?' The correct response would be something along the lines of, 'north-nor'-east, in the middle distance'. But if you don't know which way north is, it's impossible to get past a simple 'hello'.

Take a moment to mull this over. The language forces the speaker to remain orientated *at all times*—inside or outside, night or day, stationary or moving, clear or foggy, in familiar or unfamiliar locations. Without doing this, they can't share even the most basic information. And if someone screams that a crocodile is approaching fast from the south-west, not knowing your directions could escalate into a life-or-death scenario.

It's more than a matter of communication, though. Languages that force constant awareness of direction foster a profound difference in navigational ability, orientation and spatial knowledge.

If an English speaker were to learn a language that relied on cardinal directions, we'd likely look for clues in the environment to help us establish direction. Native speakers don't pause in mid conversation and contemplate the sun—they intuitively know where north, south, west and east are.

By chance, a man was documented telling friends about the time his boat capsized in stormy and shark-infested water, and he swam almost five kilometres to shore. More remarkable than his survival, though, was that he retold the story using cardinal directions. He described jumping off the western side of the boat while his companion flung himself off the east. They saw a big shark swimming north.

It gets better, though. The same man was filmed telling the same tale, years later. Not only did the cardinal directions match the previous footage, but the spontaneous hand gestures that indicated the direction the boat capsized matched his orientation on both occasions. Retelling the story in his language meant encoding the cardinal directions as a part of the experience.

We hear stories like these and think of individuals with extraordinary abilities. But for a speaker of geographic languages, it's entirely ordinary. It's no supernatural gift—it's simply language shaping what we focus on.

The number of words and how frequently we use them also reveals cultural values.

French is an excellent language for appreciating food in lip-smacking detail. Mongolian has a solid chunk of the language dedicated to discussing animals, which makes sense given their pastoralist bent. And learning Japanese involves learning how to say 'please' and 'thank you' in several thousand variations, depending on the situation, who you're addressing and various cultural subtleties — it's all about politeness.

It makes sense that we'd have fewer words for the things we think about least, and would tend to think about them less as a result. Not having words for a concept doesn't make us *unable* to think about it; it simply *limits* our ability, and certainly makes it more difficult, to discuss it.

At work, what areas do we want to draw attention to? Is it people, quality or innovation? Encoding these values into our vernacular forces us to remain aware of them constantly, improving our performance as a result.

**Languages that force constant awareness of direction foster a profound difference in navigational ability, orientation and spatial knowledge.**

## The consideration of cultural context versus literal translation

Perhaps the biggest challenge to producing a truly shared language is ensuring meaning is correctly conveyed when communicating with people from different cultures and subcultures, and with native speakers of different languages.

While words can be translated literally, this certainly doesn't ensure the same meaning is conveyed. Cultural context plays a massive role in the way words are interpreted. Communicating like a native speaker means learning the unique cultural codes, behaviours and customs encoded into the language, as well as the language itself.

In an interview in *The New Yorker*, one of renowned Japanese author Haruki Murakami's regular translators, Jay Rubin, was asked to identify the most untranslatable element of Murakami's work. Rubin's response: 'everything'.

The pronoun 'I' seems like a simple concept to English speakers, but in Japanese there are various forms (*watashi, boku*), each conveying different identity, etiquette and level of formality. Simply, using a single personal pronoun limits meaning.

English speakers also value specificity, whereas the Japanese language derives beauty from indirectness. To us, a literal word-for-word translation seems vague and ambiguous, the meaning obscure. Yet to a Japanese speaker, it's the implied and unmentioned that matters most. Subjects are left out of sentences, vernacular sounds and onomatopoeia are used to suggest meaning. It's almost impossible to replicate in English—it simply doesn't translate.

Poet Charles Simic summarises the follies of translation beautifully: 'It's that pigheaded effort to convey in the words of another language not only the literal meaning of a poem but an alien way of seeing things.'

**Yes, hate to break this to you guys, but she's saying those bison are actually dead. Or tired. Yeah. They are just very, very tired. Probably just sleeping, guys.**

Writer Umberto Eco proposed that every culture can be studied using Semiotics, the study of signs and symbols and their meanings. He warned that our messages can be interpreted entirely differently from what was intended when we don't share the same language, belief system or culture, an idea known as aberrant decoding.

When we look at cave paintings, most of us see a herd of bison, the ground trembling under their hooves in their triumphant escape from the hunters behind. However, psychologist Margaret Abercrombie argues that our cultural values towards living animals have resulted in an aberrant decoding of the pictograms.

The people who used this language had a very different set of values. Pre-vegan, pre-vegetarian, pre-farm, pre-abattoir, pre-supermarket, their lives depended on the hunt ... and the kill. If we look closer at the bison in the paintings, Abercrombie says, we see they're actually lying on their sides. Yes, hate to break this to you guys, but she's saying those bison are actually dead. Or tired. Yeah. They are just very, very tired. Probably just sleeping, guys.

Heck, our affiliations to various subcultures mean we don't just need to consider different languages and regional cultures; we need to be aware of translating meaning to different roles, generations and even genders.

## Zora and Randy build safety greatness

Last we caught up with Zora and Randy, they were building safety greatness on a foundation of three driving emotions: *care*, *courage* and *pride*.

Now, Zora and Randy have plenty of experience between them. They understood their workforce was predominantly male and prone to using blunt, technical language punctuated by the occasional expletive. They also knew that if they were to waltz onto site and start plastering the place with posters about care, courage and pride, they'd likely be met with some resistance.

So they took the three driving emotions and asked their people to unpack them into language that came naturally. They asked what each of the three driving emotions could look like on site, and what a conversation based on them would be.

These discussions produced absolute gold. For example, Zora and Randy discovered that for their workforce, *care* meant being part of a team where 'there are no strangers here'. They not only transformed the emotions from abstract to concrete language, but translated them into their people's vernacular. They ensured the driving emotions made sense in the unique context of their workplace.

When the Building Safety Greatness collateral rolled out on site, the colloquial language connected with everyone. It ensured the right conversations happened to put change in motion.

# How to speak...
# language

### Idea #20: Shape the shared language

A shared language holds so much possibility for influencing perspective, improving performance in certain areas and strengthening culture. It's not a quick fix or an easy win. It takes time and constant nurturing, but the rewards are there for anyone willing to invest the time and effort.

To shape the shared language, we can:

- Encode our cultural values. We need the right words to communicate what matters.

- Ensure our technical language, jargon and acronyms are improving speed and comprehension, not causing confusion. Change the words where necessary.

- Identify the areas we want to focus on. This might be people, customers, safety, success, quality, collaboration or innovation. Incorporating these into our language draws our attention, influences our perspective and, as a result, improves performance.

- Consider and define the categories we divide and group things into. Putting things into the same category makes us think of them as similar; placing them into different categories forces us to see them as unique. Organisations are full of categories, but these don't necessarily need to be set in stone. We can redefine categories to change people's perceptions. We can avoid using them in our messaging when it doesn't serve us.

- Create metaphors for important cultural elements. Connecting one concept to another influences the way we think about it. In some instances, we might need to break the typical metaphors (such as time and money) to shift people's perspective.

- Foster inclusion through a shared language with common cultural codes, but allow for different dialects. There's no one-size-fits-all approach to language, but considering dialect avoids emphasising differences and exacerbating existing divisions.

- Be wary of the cultural permissions mantras, maxims and catch-cries set. These can quickly translate into behaviours beyond what we intended.

- Let it evolve naturally. We can't force people to use a whole new language tomorrow simply by bludgeoning them with a brand book or culture manual. We need to introduce it slowly and carefully, let it grow organically. Language is guided most by leaders, but it's influenced by everyone.

## Idea #21: Translate effectively

Translation is crucial for global cross-cultural communication, but it can be just as applicable for different generations, professions and even genders. This is particularly important when communicating our purpose, vision, values and mission.

To translate effectively, we can:

- Understand that different cultures and subcultures, genders and generations interpret meaning based on different cultural codes and contexts.

- Push past word-for-word translations and communicate intent and meaning. This means understanding how concepts are interpreted by each culture/subculture, and adapting our messaging accordingly. This may mean producing multiple messages, each potentially using very different language.

- Understand that our linguistic style influences how we're perceived, and how we perceive others. We need to be able to adapt our style depending on the audience. We also need to look past our own preferences to judge others fairly.

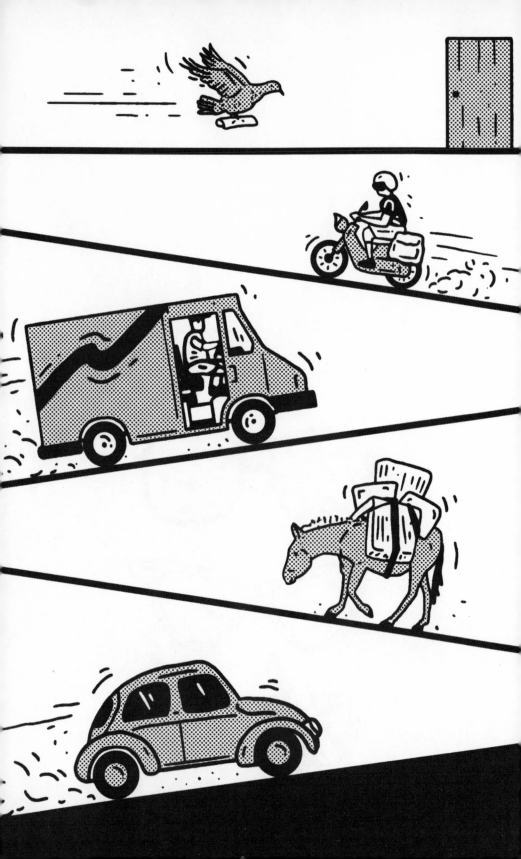

# Modes
## The perks of matching the mode to the message

Arguably one the most wonderful aspects of being human is the sheer diversity the classification allows. If a cheetah had stripes you'd call it a tiger. Paint stripes on a horse, you'd call it a zebra. Not so, though, with humans.

Oh, the variety of characteristics and traits the term can comprise. Creatures of almost infinite shape, size, colour and configuration. With all these differences, you'd be mad to assume a generic, one-size-fits-all approach to communication could possibly engage *everyone*, right? Yet this is exactly what typical workplace communication does. The same mediums, the same message, the same mode, copy and pasted to the entire organisation.

Efficient? Indeed. But engaging? Perhaps we can do better.

To communicate in a human way, to gain attention, influence and engage those around us, we need to understand the subtle yet important differences in the way various delivery modes influence our communication. When do we hit the keyboard and write an email rather than getting up on our soapbox to give a speech? Understanding when and how to use each mode to our advantage is a critical skill.

### The mode can be a shortcut to attention

Simply choosing the right delivery mode for our message increases our chances of getting people's attention. A wordy email sent to someone out on a job is likely to get skimmed at best or ignored at worst. Sending a quick text on a messaging platform would be a far better way to ensure it's seen and acknowledged. An obvious example, yet it illustrates the difference choosing the right delivery mode can make.

## The mode makes a difference

Each mode has inherent strengths and weaknesses. Correctly matching the mode to the message increases the likelihood of its connecting and making a difference. Moving people to action is far more likely to be achieved through a rousing Churchillian speech than through a multi-page memo. Similarly, the telephone isn't the best mode for teaching someone how to use a complex piece of equipment.

## The modes we use shape our organisation

Imagine trying to build an agile, fast-paced organisation using only traditional mail. Futile! Our communication modes contribute to more than attention or influence; they shape the way our organisation works.

## Spoken language

Here's a fun fact for the next time you find yourself struggling to resurrect a dull conversation: Humans began speaking long before we wrote down our words. While evidence of speech function can be found in the bones of early humans galivanting around Africa 1.5 to 1.9 million years ago, the earliest example of writing, usually attributed to the Sumerians, is dated to a relatively recent 3200 BC.

Even now, we have a bias towards speech. We learn to speak before learning to read or write, and most kids can speak a language well enough to communicate by the time they're three years old. Though most don't have anything interesting to say for the next 15–20 years. Just sayin'. 

While literacy rates have improved in most developed countries, around 14 per cent of the global population still communicates exclusively using speech.

More than any other mode, conversations are the way we prefer to communicate and connect. Even the most introverted among us has a reluctant fondness for a decent chat.

Getting into the technicals, speech is typically spat out in short, seven- to ten-word bursts. It's immediate rather than reflective, which is the reason even the smartest folk can say not-so-smart things before thinking. It's often delightfully loose, casual, full of repetitions, incomplete sentences, self-corrections and interruptions.

While we separate written words with spaces for clarity, few folk enunciate casual speech as clearly. For speed and fluidity we slur 'did you eat?' into a very different-sounding 'jueet?' Yes, what comes out of our mouths could be written as a whole new language (speshly inastraya). For this reason, spoken communication often feels less formal than written communication, unless we write phonetically.

Because speaking generally involves at least one other person (unless you're fond of a sneaky soliloquy or monologue), feedback from whoever is listening continuously influences what we say next. It allows us to read situations and shape our communication accordingly. We can ensure comprehension through clarifications.

Speaking also relies heavily on unspoken context and shared knowledge. Where and when we have a conversation makes a difference. We can leave things unsaid or imply them indirectly.

Of all the communication modes, speech naturally allows the most nuance. It isn't only about the words, it's also the way we deliver them. We can determine how our words are interpreted simply by the way we say them, a combination of speech and body language known as *paralanguage*.

Gestures, intonation, inflection, emphasis, volume, rhythm, speed, pitch, tone, pauses, movement, visual cues, timing and timbre—all convey additional context, meaning and emotion, communicating more information than the words alone.

We can string words together quickly and energetically to convey urgency or enthusiasm. We can slow the pace to create a mood that's relaxed or considered. We can adopt a measured, structured style that uses longer sentences and incorporates more ideas, to demonstrate credibility, authority and expertise.

The measured delivery of 'Bond ... *James* Bond' is no coincidence. Pausing between his words demonstrates credibility. Curling his voice down in the last syllable conveys confidence and competence. A slight Scottish lisp is icing on the cake.

Finally, the nature of speech means that words disappear once spoken. Unless it's documented on video or audio recording, speech is far less permanent than writing. We're busy and distracted, our memory prone to error, making it less likely we'll remember spoken content accurately in the long term.

Advantages of speech:

- Establishes connection and cultivates relationships
- Conveys nuanced meaning and emotion
- Can adapt message on the fly by reading response

Disadvantages of speech:

- Temporary — can be forgotten if not documented
- Easy to say the wrong thing accidentally

## A brief mention of the unspoken

Let's not punish the unspoken. It's estimated that 80 to 90 per cent of meaning is conveyed non-verbally. These are signals that complement speech, adding meaning and context to what we say.

Non-verbals can be used to reinforce or contradict our words, convey emotion, define the relationship with the people we're talking to, provide feedback when someone else is speaking or regulate the flow of conversation.

This type of communication is often instinctual and far harder to consciously control than the words we use. Which also makes it a more accurate representation of a person's thoughts and feelings compared with what they might be saying. *Your words say one thing, but your face says another...*

Yes, actions certainly do speak louder than words.

Non-verbal communication includes physical movement, facial expressions, body postures, gestures, oculesics (eyes), haptics (touching), proxemics (distance), physiological changes and breathing.

All are important, though breathing particularly so. It indicates our mood and influences our state of mind. High, shallow, rapid breathing releases chemicals that drive the fight-or-flight response. It's typically associated with nervousness, anxiety, anger or excitement. Conversely, slower, deeper breathing makes us relax and conveys confidence.

The term 'body language' is deceptive, as it accounts for only a small component of non-verbal communication. Unlike sign language, which is a complete language system capable of comprehensive communication, body language is open to interpretation.

While some non-verbals are universal, many vary between countries and cultures. Eye contact is considered a sign of trustworthiness in many Western cultures, but can be construed as disrespectful in some Indigenous cultures.

The only grudging consensus is that seven emotions are universally obvious in our expressions: happiness, surprise, fear, anger, contempt, disgust and sadness. Though recent evidence suggests pride and shame may also be universal.

Advantages of the unspoken:

• Conveys emotion — strengthens our words

• Adds context and meaning — reinforces our words

• Allows us to give ongoing feedback without speaking (nodding, cocking head, shaking head)

• Regulates the flow of conversation

• Defines our relationships with others

• Can be used to interpret how others really feel — a more accurate representation than their words

Disadvantages of the unspoken:

- Can be a giveaway to others when we don't believe what we're saying

- Can be prone to unintended miscommunication due to cultural differences

## Formal speeches and spoken performances

Since our beginnings, stories, songs and rituals have been passed on orally to preserve them. Yet even with higher literacy rates today, we remain enchanted by spoken traditions like speeches, theatre, news and storytelling.

While formal speeches and spoken conversations may seem similar, speeches actually have more in common with written language. Like writing, speeches tend to be delivered to larger and more diverse audiences. This means that unlike conversations, we need to establish context and common ground.

Speeches also require more precision and clarity than a casual chat. Once spoken, words can't be retracted (unfortunately). So while we can apologise, qualify or explain, it's better to get them right when they first leave our mouth.

Effective formal speeches balance the concise and considered language used in writing with the engaging and nuanced delivery of speech.

Advantages of formal speeches:

- Compelling and engaging when done well

- Shared experience of hearing a message as a group

- Motivate, inspire or move a group towards a common purpose

Disadvantages of formal speeches:

- Saying the wrong thing requires awkward clarifications or apologies

- Can be prone to misinterpretation
- Need to be written specifically and delivered well for them to be engaging

## Written language

Compared with speech, written language is a more considered, contemplative and deliberative mode of communication. It has the potential to be concise, precise and detailed, but also requires focus and effort to read, consider and process.

The writer(s) (in this case, us) can write and rewrite content to get it exactly the way we want it. The reader (in this case, you), has the option to read quickly or slowly, pause to consider the content, or reread to clarify. In this way, both the writer and the reader control the pace. Together, we dance to the same tune but an entirely different beat.

Because we're here and you're there (wherever 'there' is — we hope it's somewhere tropical, where cocktails are festively crowned by tiny, coloured umbrellas) ... Where were we? Ahh yes, because we're sadly separated by time and space, context becomes important. We need context to ensure meaning is accurately conveyed to an audience that may not share the same background information or knowledge. This is especially important given that written communication can be around for centuries. [*Tugs at collar and gulps*]

Unlike conversations, feedback is delayed. We can't seek or provide immediate clarification, nor ensure everyone reading understands exactly what we mean. This means we need to be clear and unambiguous to ensure important content is understood.

Written language often feels more formal than spoken language. This is partly because it's bound by more rules and conventions than speech. Where speaking has a more nuanced delivery, writing relies on punctuation, hierarchy, structure and visual elements to aid comprehension and convey meaning. This standardisation allows us to understand writing right back to the 1400s.

Formality isn't just a result of structure, though; it's also a hangover hauled into the present from times long past.

In previous centuries, literacy rates were much lower. Only the educated upper classes, professional bodies, government and universities used written language to communicate, and they tended to write as they spoke—formally. Meanwhile, most of the working classes were barely able to read, let alone write, and, as a result, their tendency towards colloquial speech never translated into written language.

These days, though, things are different. There's a far higher literacy rate in our workforce than a century ago. And this shift, along with new forms of messaging, has brought a delightful trend towards the informal. However, higher education still drums formal, academic writing into us, and organisations continue to perpetuate the formal written prose from centuries past. We often hear this justified as *professional*. We could just as easily call it *irrelevant*. 😊

We're no longer writing exclusively for the academics and upper class—we're writing for the people. And few of us choose to use formal language when communicating with our friends. If we want our writing to connect, it should celebrate the glorious colloquialisms and informalities that abound in everyday vernacular.

**Together, we dance to the same tune but an entirely different beat.** Finally, there's email. This is possibly the single biggest complaint we hear when it comes to communication at work. The problem tends to be when it's treated like traditional written language. It's often used as a catch-all solution to conveying everything from lengthy technical content to short, informal texts.

Perhaps if we actually had to haul out a pen and paper every time we wanted to send a message, we'd be a lot more discerning with our words. It's worth considering what we share in email, and what gets shared using other delivery modes and mediums.

Advantages of written language:

- Communicates detailed or in-depth information
- Can switch style to differentiate, or appeal to a specific demographic

- Allows recipients to read/reread at their own pace to understand content

- Provides a paper trail

Disadvantages of written language:

- Requires time, effort and focus to consume and process content

- Can feel more formal and less engaging to many people

- Can't guarantee comprehension because feedback is delayed

## Texting, messaging and asynchronous communication

Texting emerged with new technology and the communication mediums it enabled: text messaging, SMS, IM, and chat platforms like WhatsApp and Messenger. For the first time, we were able to produce and deliver written messages almost as quickly as our thoughts.

We're no longer writing letters for delivery a week later, friends. We're in the same moment, with shared context, gaining immediate feedback. And if you're thinking that all sounds a lot like spoken language — you're bang on there. Yes, despite the written medium, texting is actually much closer to speech than writing.

Linguist John McWhorter describes texting as 'fingered speech', and it certainly flairs with all the delicious looseness of spoken language. A flagrant disregard for conventions like punctuation or capitalisation. Fraught with abbreviations, aberrations and other grammatical abominations. The cravings of conversation, but controlled at our own pace.

However, while even our grandparents enthusiastically adapted, many organisations are still stuck in a pre-text bubble. We're not advocating grammatical anarchy, but it's time to shift our perception of what written communication should be.

This means embracing new asynchronous communication mediums like Slack, Yammer and the myriads of others that have no doubt popped up between our writing and your reading this book. It means using them in the way they're meant to be used. It might feel strange to loosen the reins in a work environment, but you need only look at an automated text message from a bank or telco to see how odd and unnatural perfectly formed language is in this mode. The style jars peculiar, so cold and impersonal compared with the homely warmth of a little colloquialism.

Advantages of texting and messaging:

- Fast to put together and instant delivery—well suited for quick, informal messages
- Loose and colloquial—easy to consume
- Promotes conversations rather than one-way messaging

Disadvantages of texting and messaging:

- Transient—easy for the recipient to miss important details
- Not suited for detailed information

## Visual language

Visual languages are written, but don't use letters or words in a typical sense.

These languages have spanned centuries and continents, evident in cave paintings, ancient Sumerian cuneiform, Egyptian hieroglyphs, Mayan glyphs, Chinese kanji and various indigenous cultures, including Australian and American.

Today, visual language systems are everywhere we look, from signage and packaging to the internet and mobile devices. We live in a fast-paced and ever-shrinking world, where visual languages allow us to convey messages and ideas instantly, simply, clearly and unambiguously. They transcend geographical and literacy barriers.

Many systems have become standardised, becoming truly universal languages. Some concepts have become so linked to certain symbols that they can communicate meaning without using words. The cross, the swastika, the caduceus (medical symbol), the skull and crossbones—these have been imbued with centuries of ideology and emotion.

There are several common categories of visual languages, though the boundaries between them frequently blur. Let's look at each in a little more detail.

## Logograms

Logograms are abstract symbols that represent entire words or phrases.

Kanji is a written language used by Chinese, Japanese and Korean speakers and composed of 47 035 logograms (though only 4000 to 5000 are used by the average person).

If the name didn't give it away, logograms are commonly known in the business world as logos. These are typically used in branding to build consumer recognition. When we see the swoosh, we think, *Nike, just do it.* When we see the golden arches, our salivary glands start screaming for McDonald's fries.

## Pictograms

Pictograms (or pictographs) are symbols that literally depict objects.

These include airport wayfinding, road signage, safety and hazard signage, recycling and waste symbols, and clothing care instructions. Their literal nature means we're likely to understand their meaning even if we haven't seen them before, and no matter what language we speak.

## Ideograms

Ideograms are symbols that communicate ideas or concepts. They can literally resemble an object, or use abstract forms and colours.

For example, depending on the context in which it's used, a light-bulb symbol often represents ideas, while a lightning bolt represents electricity or energy. We understand that any object inside a red circle with a line through it is forbidden. Similarly, we know to be cautious of any object shown inside a triangle.

## Emoji

When you regularly receive emails littered with emoji from your 85-year-old grandmother, you know the language system is legit.

Essentially, emojis are just pictograms, not dissimilar from kanji, hieroglyphs or bison cavorting across prehistoric cave walls. However, the rapid and relatively recent emergence of this language makes it worthy of special attention.

Long before our devices had the graphical power to display the Pile of Poop emoji (💩), we were forced to punch various combinations of letters, numbers and punctuation marks to create crude pictures and faces to communicate emotion ¯\\_(ツ)_/¯. These primitive emoticons were the precursor to modern emojis.

Today, emoji is not only integrated into our native languages; it's becoming a legitimate language system in its own right.

Linguistic professor Vyv Evans describes it as Britain's fastest-growing language, and it's not surprising. Emoji pairs perfectly with technology, allowing for fast-paced communication that parallels instant messaging and character constraints on social media platforms.

Casper Grathwohl, president of Oxford Dictionaries, summed up the appeal of emoji perfectly in his justification for awarding 😂 (Face with Tears of Joy) their Word of the Year for 2015:

> *Traditional alphabet scripts have been struggling to meet the rapid-fire, visually focused demands of 21st century communication. It's not surprising that a pictographic script like emoji has stepped in to fill those gaps — it's flexible, immediate, and infuses tone beautifully.*

However, while a love of laughing until crying is almost universal, a survey conducted by HighSpeedInternet.com suggests that a country's second favourite emoji might provide a more fascinating cultural insight.

Our French friends love a ♡ (Heart), which isn't surprising at all for a country with a capital known as the City of Love. South Africans are also lovers, but more of the lusty variety with a fondness for 😗 (Face Blowing a Kiss). Ireland has quite the proclivity for the 💩 (Pile of Poop). And in Australia apparently we're 😜 (Winking Face with Stuck Out Tongue) — mad as cut snakes, mates.

Disturbing sidebar: while Oxford was celebrating Face with Tears of Joy, the American Dialect Society declared 🍆 (Eggplant) their Most Notable Emoji of 2015.

Speaking of eggplants... like hand signs or any language, emojis are just as prone to misinterpretation. Their inherent ambiguity allows for flexible usage, but also meaning that varies between age groups, cultures and nationalities. Oh yes, the innocuous Eggplant is apparently **Today, emoji is not only integrated into our native languages; it's becoming a legitimate language system in its own right.** not considered a vegetarian-friendly menu option by 18- to 25-year-olds. And expressing your desire for a juicy 🍑 may not communicate exactly what you'd intended either. 😵

Advantages of visual language:

- Universally understood — commonly used systems transcend geographical and literacy barriers
- Conveys ideas and concepts quickly
- Communicates emotions (emoji)

Disadvantages of visual language:

- Some systems, like emoji, are still open to a degree of interpretation and can vary depending on demographic and context

### Manual languages and hand signs

Manual languages visually represent a written language by using our body as a means of expression.

Fingerspelling (dactylology) uses fingers and hands to represent letters and numbers. It's mainly used in deaf education or in conjunction with sign language, though it's also used by technicality-exploiting monks to avoid breaking their vows of silence.

Hand signs and gestures can substitute for words in various situations. Scuba divers use hand signs to indicate intentions that for obvious reasons can't be conveyed through speech; construction workers use them to communicate in a noisy environment.

Using them to communicate cross-culturally is fraught with the potential to offend, however, and can lead to entirely unintended consequences.

In Australia, we give the thumbs-up as a sign of approval, but in Latin America, West Africa, Greece, Sardinia, Russia and the Middle East it's considered quite rude. Beckoning someone to follow using your finger is punishable by finger-breaking in the Philippines. Fingers crossed means the same thing as the middle finger up in Vietnam. An A-OK sign is actually an a-hole sign in Greece, Turkey, Brazil and the Middle East. The peace sign can start a fight in England, but throw the satanic salute at a Buddhist monk and they'll smile at your benevolent gesture to dispel evil.

Yes, it's all very confusing. Fortunately, flicking the bird (the middle finger) is offensive in any culture, so you're still well covered there.

Advantages of manual language and hand signs:

- Allows visual communication when conversation isn't possible because of distance, noise or environment

Disadvantages of manual language and hand signs:

- Interpretation will vary dramatically, depending on demographic, culture and context

### Turn it all two-way

Here's a fascination: the word 'communication' evolved from the Latin verb *communicare*, to share. How good! *Sharing* evokes an image of people actively involved in circulating a message they care about.

Losing the feels and turning it technical, all communication requires a sender, a message and a recipient (or recipients). The process is considered successful only when the recipient not only receives but also *understands* the sender's message.

This raises an important question: how do we know our message has been not only received — but *understood*?

Irish playwright George Bernard Shaw once claimed that 'the single biggest problem in communication is the illusion that it has taken place'. And there's the rub. How many *almost*-communications are floating around at work? How many senders might be assuming their recipients chose not to act or respond, while the intended recipients never actually received or understood the message?

Obviously, we have no chance of influencing anyone if our message isn't understood.

The only way to ensure our communication connects is by turning it two-way. Effective communication isn't only about improving how we *send* messages; it's also about getting better at *receiving* them. It's amazing what we learn when we listen, how we improve when we seek a response, and how people respond when we open a conversation.

The mode we choose goes a long way towards enabling this type of interaction.

The process is considered successful only when the recipient not only receives but also *understands* the sender's message.

# How to speak...
# modes

### Idea #22: Switch perspectives

We need to become experts in empathy, masters at identifying and catering to preferences outside our own. This is how we create communication that connects and resonates.

To switch perspectives, we can:

- Begin by understanding that within our organisations there are various segments, each with its own unique characteristics and preferences.

- Understand explicitly who we're communicating with on each occasion.

- Use an activity like creating personas to help us understand the preferences of our intended recipients.

- Produce different collateral to appeal to specific segments, where necessary. The same message can be delivered using different language or mediums. Certain content may be relevant to one group, but not to another.

- Consider the advantages and disadvantages of the various modes when determining which to use.

- Stay curious about the way language is evolving, and shift our communication accordingly. This is how we create relevant messaging that connects, especially with younger generations.

## Idea #23: Turn it two-way

Wherever possible, let's make communication flow both ways. This helps us ensure our messages are received and understood, and actually have a chance of making a difference.

To turn it two-way, we can:

- Establish a rhythm of communication. These are proactive, culture-driven rituals and touchpoints, rather than the scatter-gun messaging that comes from communicating only when we want people to do something. This rhythm allows for conversations and builds relationships. It isn't about campfires and 'Kumbaya', it's about making sure everyone's on the same page and our messages are connecting.

- Encourage and create opportunities for responses to our messaging. This might mean using a two-way channel, or building feedback touchpoints into our programs.

- Ask questions rather than making statements. Questions open conversations; statements remove the opportunity to respond.

- Engage in active listening. Ask questions that seek further clarification, and show comprehension by reframing and repeating what you've just heard.

# Beware...
## The excuses for mediocrity

Oh, the resistance you'll face when you try to speak human.

The excuses for why it *can't* be done; *shouldn't* be done. The absurdities you'll hear to justify speaking the Language of Business. Unlike any other dialect, this stilted corporate prose will one day baffle linguists with its archaic form. The bastard of formal speech and writing from the turn of the 20th century, it exists ostensibly to bewilder.

Yes, if you've ever tried to push communication past predictable, chances are you've met with one of these reasons why it can't be done:

**Legal**: We have to say it like this...

**Branding**: Our brand guidelines say we need to say it like this...

**Complexity**: It's too complicated or technical to explain simply...

**Cost**: We don't have time or budget to say it better...

**Tradition**: This is how we've always said it...

**Fear**: We can't risk saying it like that...

**Professionalism**: We need to say it that way to be professional...

To put it quite bluntly, these are all terrible excuses. Whether it's a legal document, policy manual or corporate strategy, if we want attention, engagement and influence, we need to be speaking human.

So let's break these excuses down in more detail, and arm ourselves with some answers.

## Legal

*'We have to say it like this…'*

Many organisations have a warm and friendly tone… until it's time for a contract or policy. Then the vibe turns frigid. But why does legal language need to have all the personality sucked right out?

Nowhere in any legal manual we've ever come across does it specify the need for bloated, excessively syllabled, jargon-heavy, impersonal language. The assumption that The Law demands such long-winded pomposity might simply be a leftover from a time when olde-worlde scriveners were paid by the word. Needless to say, with the lure of more money, much verbiage and verbosity ensued.

So, unless we're being paid by the word, we're free to approach legal communication in a whole new way. The challenge for us, and our pals who advise us on legal matters, is to translate legislation, regulation and policy into clear and concise language that matches up with our organisation.

Yes, let's push past word count and focus on comprehension and engagement. There's such an opportunity to create better communication — simply by changing the legal language.

## Branding

*'Our brand guidelines say we need to say it like this…'*

Most companies have brand language guidelines, preached with varying degrees of fervour. These direct word choice and tone, vocabulary and attitude. They're often formulated by branding and advertising agencies almost exclusively to influence the external market by defining and differentiating the company from all the others.

While we champion a consistent and unified internal/external brand, too often these guides become The Rules. Applied over and over as an inflexible one-size-fits-all approach to internal communication, saying things in exactly the same way, day in and day out, they inevitably fade into a background hum.

Communication doesn't come from a brand or culture book, no matter how hard or frequently corporate comms bludgeon folk with it. No, language comes from the leaders; it comes from the people. It's in the daily conversations with each other and our customers and clients. It can't be fully controlled by a brand agency or single department — it lives and evolves throughout the entire organisation.

## Complexity

*'It's too complicated or technical to explain simply...'*

Remember, complexity isn't the real issue. The world is complex, humans are complex, life is complex, work is complex — *everything* is complex. We deal with complexity daily; it's naive to think we can, or should, solve complexity by eliminating the details. That's just dumbing it down, stripping the function that makes it useful.

The problem is *confusion*.

Fortunately, simplicity is actually, ironically, quite simple. The blandest technical information can be made easy to understand. The driest legal document can be made palatable. Make things easy to understand, and they'll seem simple. And when things seem simple, they become far more interesting, engaging and influential too.

## Cost

*'We don't have time or budget to say it better...'*

There's no way to sugar-coat this, mates — saying it better is almost certainly going to require more effort, more time and quite possibly more money.

But what's the point in saying anything if no-one's listening? What's the point in making any effort at all if it won't be acted on? Investing a little bit extra makes all the difference to earning attention and making a difference. The cost of mediocrity is undeniably higher.

## Tradition

*'This is how we've always said it…'*

Communication is changing, language is changing, business is changing, people are changing. Staying ahead today means staying relevant tomorrow. We must evolve — continuously.

This means shedding the shackles of tradition. Let's allow our communication to shift, consider new ways to connect with and inspire the next generations driving our organisations forwards.

## Fear

*'We can't risk saying it like that…'*

In terms of challenges, fear is one of the biggest hurdles we see at a leadership level. Fear of doing something different. Fear of putting ourselves out there. Fear of failure. Fear of causing offence. Fear of what people might say. Fear of responsibility. Fear that others will do the wrong thing. Fear of change. Fear of becoming irrelevant. Whatever it's masked as, it often comes back to fear.

Fear is responsible for many of the unnecessary layers of confusion and complication. We see it when leaders hide behind vague, stilted corporate language — ass-covering, justification, death by committee. Systems at the expense of common sense. Endless policies and procedures written in mind-numbingly dry and indecipherable prose.

This confusion multiplies as we move through levels, as each function attempts to shield themselves from risk and accountability, or to cover a lack of understanding. It's no wonder that by the time we reach the intended recipients, we're left with bloated processes and strategies, with all the human sucked right out. This isn't useful complexity, it doesn't add function or purpose — it's just confusion. And when people are confused, they lose interest and become disengaged.

**Fear is responsible for many of the unnecessary layers of confusion and complication.**

We get that this is far more challenging in practice than theory. None of these fears are unreasonable, and a culture that gives permission to do things differently — or even to fail gloriously — comes from the top. But the truly remarkable leaders we've worked with are the ones who move past fear. They're willing to do what it takes to make a difference. They bring everything back to what really matters: humans.

## Professionalism

*'We need to say it that way to be professional...'*

Of all the fears, this one deserves special attention.

*Professional.* That word—synonymous with the death of hope for creating interesting, engaging, difference-making, human work. A bastardisation of an honest word, misused to excuse ass-covering, complacent comfort in the status quo, and a lack of courage to stand behind beliefs and fight for remarkable.

'We need to engage our people, but we need it to be *professional.*'

Phrased as if human and professional were mutually exclusive. And there's the proverbial rub. But when did we become so wrapped up in these abstract notions of professionalism?

Let's begin with the birthing of the word, sometime in the 17th century. The etymology reads, verbatim: *from Middle English, from profes, adjective, having professed one's vows* [followed by some indecipherable business about professing in various languages etc. etc.] *Late Latin professus* [etc. something about a past participle of *profitēri* (which I don't think is in any way related to a profiterole) etc. etc. etc.].

Wedged between all that convoluted Latin and past participle business is a concept as simple as it is delightful: to be a professional, you commit to practising your learned profession by professing your skill to others.

If we flip dictionary pages to the *definition* of professional, we see a similar story:

1. relating to or belonging to a profession

2. engaged in a specified activity as one's main paid occupation rather than as an amateur.

Belonging to a profession. Doing your job. Simple. Honourable. Still no skeletons in professional's closet.

Or are there?

Obviously we weren't around in the 19th century—we were still just a lusty feeling in our great-great-grandparents' loins. However, all evidence points to the Victorians as the molesters of professional's honour.

Don your bonnet or top hat—we're taking a quick detour back in time to 19th century London to investigate. Picture skylines of smoke-belching chimneys thrust from squat brick factories—we're smack bang in the iron belly of the industrial revolution, where big changes are underway. For the first time, land and family name aren't the only sources of wealth. It's now possible for anyone with ambition and imagination to make their fortune from manufacturing and trading goods.

With these new industries, new roles emerged, many requiring formal education and training. And although there are no such indications in the etymology or definition, professional became synonymous with a university education. In contrast, roles with apprenticeships and on-the-job training were referred to as trades, skills or crafts.

This may sound like an unnecessary fuss over semantics; however, the association with university-educated, white-collar careers planted professional firmly in the domain of the Victorian middle class. And this is where the perversion of professional began.

With the influx of the freshly educated and newly monied, the middle class bulged in both size and influence, and the 'old' middle class were less than thrilled. Class distinctions became increasingly important—a way for the respectable, established professionals, like lawyers and doctors, to elevate themselves in the social hierarchy above the 'new' businessmen and technocrats.

Meanwhile, the men who'd risen from humble beginnings worried constantly about fitting in, cloaking their insecurities in the paraphernalia of gentility. Big houses and fine frocks, but always the fear of being found lacking by their peers.

Around this time, the Victorians took professional and added an *-ism* to it. Sounds innocuous enough, but those three little letters made an inordinate difference. Suddenly, simply practising a profession wasn't enough. It wasn't a case of being a professional or not — professional*ism* created a continuum on which your importance could be measured and compared to others.

A man's education and qualifications (where and what), title, role, income, address, attire, manners, possessions, even the nature of the profession, determined his level of professional*ism*.

If this sounds familiar, it should. Many of our current notions of professionalism — obsessions with qualifications, formality, manners, language, dress, status, materialism, and by-the-book conservative nature — can be tracked all the way back to Victorian middle-class aspirations.

Things really ramped up for the recently reborn notions of professionalism through the 20th century. The 1980s through 90s were the golden era of Human Resource departments, which accurately sums up how organisations felt about people in business at the time.

Management mostly held themselves at arm's length from their fleshy assets, shielding themselves in corner offices, behind suits, ties, cleverly indecipherable acronyms, and deadpan masks of corporate formality. Many of these leaders were company-faced powerbrokers: impersonal, unapproachable and intolerant of mistakes. And still the misplaced focus on the Victorian trappings of professionalism. Fast cars. Sharp suits. Professional was priority, human was on hiatus.

Then things changed.

Given enough time, almost everything changes. In this case, the subtlest shift in attitude to professionalism shook the whole edifice. A change brought about by new generations with drastically different ideals.

You needn't hunt much further than a tech company or start-up to see a radical new interpretation of professionalism. A relaxed and flexible attitude permeates these companies, shaping everything from clothing and culture to work hours and incentives. Workplaces are open plan — designed to encourage collaboration. Leaders are no longer found ensconced in isolated office suites on upper floors, but down in the trenches with everyone else.

Yes, gone are the days of barging into boardrooms barking curt orders and leaving. The days of the one-way, top-down, do what

I say because I said it are past. Managing the younger generations means being available and approachable, facilitating conversation and collaboration, providing ongoing feedback.

We've changed, a lot...

We've burst triumphant from the human resources era into a people, leadership and culture age. It's the renaissance of real. Human is back...

Yet many organisations stubbornly haul baggage from the century before last. Some leaders are still back with the Victorians banging away about propriety and professionalism. Professional went from a simple promise to do our best to a concept floundering for meaning in a modern workplace, wheeled out selectively by managers seeking safety in the status quo.

**The days of the one-way, top-down, do what I say because I said it are past.** So let's wind it back—past professionalism, right back to professional, where practising our profession is our first, second and third concern. As leaders, our job is to lead using whatever methods and forms of communication serve that purpose best—even if it's sharing a cat gif or Snapchat, 'professionalism' be damned.

We don't actually need to be less professional. Just the opposite. What we need to do is recalibrate the definition of professional for a modern organisation, and bring more human to our workplace interactions.

So let's begin by redefining the very bereft term for relevance in a modern workplace. Let's reframe professionalism to consider:

- *Performance*: doing our job at the highest level (not amateur)

- *Appropriateness*: focusing on what's relevant and appropriate to our company/brand, corporate culture, social culture, industry and role

- *Leadership*: providing the vision, values, tools, information and environment for others to give their best

- *Human*: never, ever at the expense of human.

Yep, doing our jobs the best we can—*that's* professional.

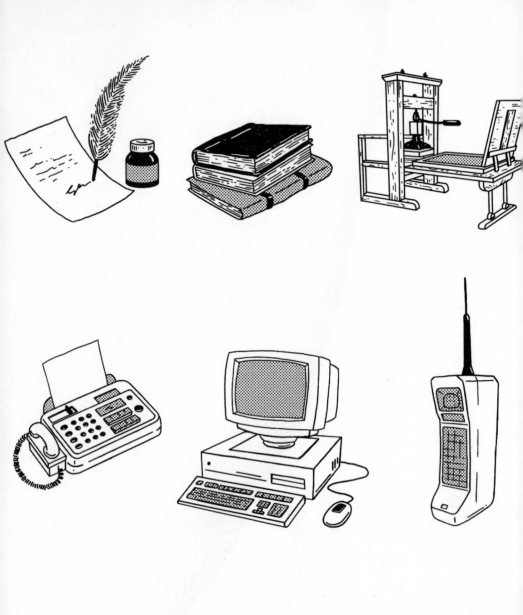

# Time, tide and the inevitability of change

As sure as tide and taxes, time marches on. And just as surely, communication evolves.

Technology often plays a major role in these shifts. Mediums like texting and character restrictions on social platforms instigated an explosion of acronyms, initialisms and entirely new visual language systems like emoji. Before that, it was the telephone that influenced the way we had conversations, or the printing press that changed our production and consumption of written content.

Even without changes to the way we communicate, language naturally evolves.

Read seven books, one from each century from the 1400s through to today, and it's obvious how much English has evolved. Even a book published in the early 1900s can take some effort to read. Alternatively, just have a conversation about pop culture with someone a decade younger, and the speed at which language changes will have you wondering WTF.

Yes, we're continually adding new words, and changing the pronunciation and meaning of existing words. One of our current favourites is 'adorkable', which means exactly what you'd assume

**By the time you read this book, new mediums will have emerged and language will have shifted.**

(an adorable dork). Meanwhile, texting words like 'lol' (laugh out loud) have transcended literal meaning to become pragmatic particles or markers of empathy—words used to fill gaps in conversation.

By the time you read this book, new mediums will have emerged and language will have shifted. While the fundamentals of being human don't change, the way we communicate does. This is why, just like our business strategy, our communication needs to evolve constantly to reflect the world outside our office walls. We should be embracing new language systems and communication mediums as opportunities to connect. These aren't passing fads, they're how we speak human.

# So ...

There we go, friends. If we've done our job right, you have all the knowledge you need to get out there and speak human and produce communication that gains attention, engages and influences.

Remember, there's no right or wrong place to start. You can dive in wherever, go as deep or shallow as you want. Heck, no matter your role or responsibilities, you can bring any or all of these strategies to your work, right now, and see a difference.

We won't promise it's going to be easy, though. Oh no, there'll be plenty of folk who'll fling all manner of well-meaning excuses for why it can't be done or shouldn't be done. But this is the work that *has* to be done if we're going to help people and organisations through the coming years.

Until we're all made redundant by robots, of course. At which time, we hope you'll join us for *How to Speak Android.*

Have you turned the power on?

Until then, chums.

# Acknowledgements

This book is built on the bones of a thousand thoughts, ideas, conversations, conferences, articles, experiments and hunches; tested, refined and retested in real-world applications.

There's no way to fairly thank all the people who've contributed in one way or another. That said, a few names demand mention.

Most of all, this book is testament to the amazing folk we've been fortunate to work with from organisations around the world. These are the leaders with a relentless drive to make a difference. They're the ones with the most at stake, and it's their courage to try something different that pushes industries and organisations forward.

To Jasmine Omar and her team, Gordon Bedford and his team, Megan Tranter, Sarah Cuscadden, Randell Fuller and countless others over the years—our warmest thanks for the opportunity to do this work with you.

To the people who've believed in and supported us over the years, and gently nudged (read: pushed) us when necessary: Jason, Kim, Darren and Alison—thank you. Particular honour and 'hat tips' (to steal his words) to Jason for opening doors and introducing us to the good folk at Wiley.

Speaking of Wiley... thanks to Lucy Raymond, Chris Shorten and the team for believing in our vision and providing a delightfully painless publishing experience replete with witty email banter. Our sincerest apologies to Jem Bates for the several thousand Oxford commas you had to remove. Thanks for tolerating Jen pursuing your felines around the garden. Oh, and for making this book better in all the right ways. We imagined editing to be an angst-ridden process. It was not.

We continue to be grateful for the support and talent of our team, past and present, at Jaxzyn. To our current crew—Bojana, Nadeen, Kenia, Tim, Jess, Kerrie and Narelle, along with frequent collaborators Samwise, Barry P, Koi, Keri, Dave from IP Assembly, and AK and Justin at WMS—you guys are the greatest. Thanks so much to all of you for sharing this adventure with us. Special mention to Barry P for the ridiculous(ly wonderful) illustrations scattered throughout this book.

Finally, gratitude and love to our families and friends who we've neglected terribly while building Jaxzyn and bringing *How to Speak Human* to life. Shout-outs to The Triple Denim Cluuurb, the PBC Sandwich Cluuurb, Lip My Stocking, Miss 'im and the Currumbin Nature Trekking Society (CNTS). Thanks for not culling us from your friendship circles and loving us for all our flaws. We are, after all, only human …

# Index

active listening 165
active vs passive voice 108–109
advertising and marketing 3–4,
  22, 34, 81–82, 83, 87
affect labelling 79
anticipation 17–25
  —attention 17–18, 19, 23
  —brain structure and
    function 21
  —curiosity 21
  —definition 17
  —destroying 17–18
  —emotions, heightening
    20–21
  —examples 19–20, 30
  —expectations, managing
    18–19, 21–22, 24
  —influence 17, 18–19, 24
  —mindset, influencing 18–19
  —networking 20
  —pace, controlling 23
  —practical ideas 23–24
  —shopping 21
  —surprise 30, 34–35
  —using 18–19
anticipatory thinking 24
attention 177
  —anticipation 17–18, 19, 23
  —complexity 95, 97,
    101, 104
  —curiosity 1, 2, 3, 4, 5–7, 15
  —emotions 78, 82

  —habituation 57, 58, 59, 60,
    61, 62
  —humour 88, 89, 91
  —language 128–129, 132,
    138, 141, 144
  —mediocrity 167, 169
  —modes of delivery 149–150,
    160
  —narratives 74
  —surprise 27, 28, 29, 34, 37,
    38
  —visual 41, 42, 43, 44, 46,
    47–48, 53, 54
  —words 108, 128–129

body language 151, 153; *see
  also* unspoken language
brain-bonding 69–70
brain structure and function
  —anticipation 21
  —curiosity 8, 10
  —emotions 78–79, 81
  —habituation 57–58
  —learning 58
  —narratives 67–68
  —surprise 29
  —visual sense 41, 44
branding
  —as an excuse 167, 168–169
  —habituation 61–62
  —internal vs external 43,
    48–49, 54, 61–62
  —visuals and 48–50

cautions *see* problems to be
aware of change, inevitability
of 175–176
clickbait 3
cognitive
—burden 101–104
—coupling 69–70
—framing 24, 118
colour, use of 43, 45
Commonwealth Games 2018,
Gold Coast 17–18
communication *see also*
complexity; language and
perception; mediocrity,
excuses for; modes of
delivery; names; Style guides;
visual language; words
—ambiguity, eliminating 102
—audience 90–91
—avoiding complexity 95–105
—changing 30
—cognitive burden 101–104
—content 98, 100–101
—context 98–99, 101
—effective 62, 111
—emotions and 77–78
—excuses for poor 167–174
—habituation 57, 59–60
—incompleteness 104
—jargon 49, 99, 102, 107,
112, 113, 115, 129, 134,
144, 168
—learning 27, 30–31, 32
—non-verbal 151–154
—purpose 97, 90–91, 149
—relevance 99–100, 101
—sequence 104
—simplicity 97–98, 102
—simplicity vs minimalism
99–100
—structure and order 104

—two-way 162–163, 165
—visual vs verbal 103–104
complexity, problems with
95–105
—attention 95, 97, 101, 104
—brain structure and function
103–104, 105
—cognitive burden 101–104
—content 98, 100–101
—context 98–99, 101
—dealing with 96–97
—decision-making 101–104
—incompleteness 104
—influence 95, 97
—language 102–102
—preparation 95–96
—recognition vs recall 105
—relevance 99–100, 101
—sequence 104
—simplicity 97–98
—simplicity vs minimalism
99–100, 102
—structure and order 104
—visual vs verbal 103–104
consistency 48–49, 54, 61–62
curiosity 1–15, 17, 19, 101
—advertising 3–4
—anticipation 21
—attention, drawing 1, 2, 3, 4,
5–7, 15
—benefits of 1–3
—brain structure and
function 8
—defined 1
—engagement 3, 7, 18, 19, 21
—examples 4–5, 6–7, 8–9,
10, 12
—incompleteness 12
—influence 1, 3–4, 6–7
—learning 1, 2–3, 5, 7–8,
9–10, 11, 13, 101
—memory and recall 9–10

—mystery, using 13
—novelty 14
—practical ideas 12–15
—relationships and 2–3
—surprise and 30
—threats to 10–11
—unpredictability 15
—variation in 3
curiosity gap 3–6, 12

decision-making 81–82,
  101–104
disappointment 22

emoji 160–161
emotional intelligence 77
emotions 77–85
—attention 78, 82
—behaviour change 81–84
—benefits 78
—brain structure and function
  78–79, 81
—communication 77–78
—connection 78
—examples 80–81, 84
—heightening 20–21
—influence 78, 82
—leading with 85
—learning 77, 78, 81–84, 85
—mindfulness 79–80, 81, 85
—negative vs positive 81–84, 85
—physiological cues 83–84
—practical ideas 85
—purchasing decisions 81–82
—regulation 79, 85
—words, relationship with
  78–81
emotive language 109–110
engagement 177
—complexity 95, 96, 97, 101
—curiosity 3, 7, 18, 19, 21
—humour 87, 90

—long-term 28–29
—mediocrity 167, 168, 170,
  171
—modes of delivery 149, 154,
  155, 157
—names 121
—narratives 65, 66, 67, 71, 73
—surprise 27, 28–29, 33, 42,
  47, 50, 54
Enron 128
examples
—aged care and story-telling
  66–67
—anticipation 19–20, 30
—communication 165
—culture change and language
  130–132
—curiosity 8–9, 10, 12, 14
—elbow licking 6–7
—humour 90–91
—innovation and narratives 72
—managing emotions 80–81
—metrics manual deck of cards
  43, 44
—mode of delivery 164
—Mya and the Blarney Stone
  8–9, 10, 12, 14, 19–20, 30
—positive emotions, using 84
—quiet achievers and narratives
  70
—rabbits campaign 4–5, 12
—safe design course name 121
—safety campaign 31–32
—safety program and language
  143
—surprise 30, 31–32
—visual appeal 43, 44, 47
—visual guide to safety 47
—visuals and branding 49–50
—visuals and corporate change
  49–50
—watermelon drop 31–32

expectation(s) 19
— managing 19, 21–22, 24
— surprise and 28
— unrealistic 10–11

failure, fear of 11
Field Guide for sales reps,
   Liam's 80–81, 90–91

habits, forming 57
habituation 57–63, 92
— attention 57, 58, 59, 60, 61,
   62, 74
— brain structure and function
   57–58
— branding 61–62
— communication 57, 59–60
— explained 57
— implicit vs explicit mind 58
— learning 58, 59
— speed of 59–60
— Style Guides 61–62
— unpredictability 60–61
happiness 21, 22
health campaign 6–7
hero's journey 71–72
high-reference language
   109–110
hippocampal-SN/VTA loop 29
Human Resources names
   123, 124
humour 87–93
— age differences 92, 93
— appeal of 88–91
— attention 88, 89, 91
— benefits 87–88
— brain structure and function
   88–89
— culture 88, 92
— examples 90–91
— influence 88
— laughter 88–89
— learning 87, 91
— practical ideas 93
— risk 87, 91–92
— social function 88, 89
— theories of 89–90
— types of 89–90, 93
— variations in 92, 93

ideas, practical
— anticipation 23–24
— curiosity 12–15
— emotions 85
— humour 93
— language 144–146
— modes of delivery 164–165
— names 124
— narratives 73–74
— surprise 36–38
— visual sense 51–54
— words 114–115
ideograms 159
illustrations, use of 47
incongruity theory of
   laughter 89
influence 177
— anticipation 17, 18–19, 24
— complexity 95, 97
— curiosity 1, 3–4
— emotions 78, 82
— humour 88
— language 128, 129,
   130–131, 131–132, 135,
   137, 138–139, 144, 145,
   146
— mediocrity 167, 168
— modes of delivery 149, 150,
   151, 153, 163, 169
— names 117–118, 119, 120,
   122, 124
— narratives 69, 73, 74

—surprise 54
—visual 41, 54
—words 101, 109–110, 111, 112

jargon 49, 99, 102, 107, 112, 113, 115, 129, 134, 144, 168
journaling 81, 90–91

language and perception *see also* communication; modes of delivery; names; visual language; word choice
—attention 128–129, 132, 138, 141, 144
—behaviour 129
—brain structure and function 68–69
—categories 136–138
—cave paintings 142–143
—cultural identity 127
—culture change program 130
—cultures and subcultures 127–128, 129–132, 144
—directions, naming 139–140
—effects 68, 127, 128–129, 132
—emotions 78–81
—examples 130–131, 143
—focus 138–141
—indirect 103
—influence 128, 129, 130–131, 131–132, 135, 137, 138–139, 144, 145, 146
—learning 133–134, 135, 136–138, 139, 140, 140, 141, 150, 163
—linguistic influence 131–132
—metaphors 134–136
—numbers and maths 133–134

—practical ideas 144–146
—recall 132
—shared 129–131, 144–145
—thought, culture and 131–132
—time concepts 134–136, 137–138
—tone 130
—varieties 108–113
—translation 141–143, 146
—variations between languages 131–138, 141–143
learning
—babies 30–31
—brain structure and function 58
—complexity 102
—curiosity 1, 2–3, 5, 7–8, 9–10, 11, 13, 101
—emotions and 77, 78, 81–84, 85
—habituation 58, 59
—humour 87, 91
—language 133–134, 135, 136–138, 139, 140, 140, 141, 150, 163
—names 120, 121–122, 124
—narratives 65, 66, 67, 73
—surprise and 27, 30–31, 32
—visual 44
loaded language 109–110
logograms 159

mediocrity, excuses for 167–174
—attention 167, 169
—branding 167, 168–169
—complexity 167, 169
—cost 167, 169
—fear 167, 170
—influence 167, 168
—legal 167, 168

mediocrity *(Cont'd)*
—professionalism 167,
   171–174
—tradition 167, 170
memory and recall
—curiosity 9–10
—language 132
—names 120
—recognition vs 105
—visual sense 45
metaphors 134–136
mindfulness 79–80, 81, 85,
   90–91
modes of delivery 149–165
—asynchronous
   communication 157–158
—attention 149–150, 160
—body language 151, 153
—effects 149–150
—formal speeches 154–155
—hand signs 161–162
—influence 149, 150, 151,
   153, 163, 169
—manual languages 161–162
—messaging 157–158
—origins of speech 150
—practical ideas 164–165
—sign language 153
—speech performance
   154–155
—spoken language 150–152
—texting 157–158
—two-way communication
   162–163, 165
—unspoken language 151,
   152–154
—visual language 158–162,
   175
—written language 155–157
Mya and the Blarney Stone
   examples 8–9, 10, 12, 14,
   19–20, 30

names 117–125
—categorisation 120–121, 122,
   124
—categorisation, pros and cons
   120–121
—children's 119
—effects 117, 118
—engagement 121
—examples 119
—Human Resources 123, 124
—influence 117–118, 119,
   120, 122, 124
—impact of 118–119
—learning 120, 121–122, 124
—perspective 122
—practical ideas 124
—relationships, showing 123
—recall 120
narratives (story-telling) 35,
   65–76, 101
—benefits 66, 67, 69, 71
—brain-bonding 69–70
—brain structure and function
   67–69
—cognitive coupling 69–70
—crafting 70–72, 73
—culture building 66
—examples 66–67, 70, 73
—explained 65–66
—hero's journey 71–72
—influence 69, 73, 74
—language processing 68
—learning 65, 66, 67, 73
—neural entrainment 68–69
—person-centricity 67
—practical ideas 73–74
—senses, engaging 67–68
—sharing 73
—visual forms 74
negativity 81–84
networking 20
neural entrainment 68–69

neuroscience *see* brain structure
and function
numbers and maths 133–134

paralanguage *see* body language
peak-end theory customer
service 33
perceptual defence 34
pictograms 159
Play with Care strategy 47
positivity bias 34
PowerPoint, poor use of 42, 59,
65, 71, 95
preparation 95–96
problems to be aware of 57–63,
95–105, 167–174
professionalism 167, 171–174
purchasing decisions 81–82

relief theory of laughter 89
repetitive tasks 58
rhetorical language 110
routine, comfort with 32–33

selective deception 34
shock *see also* surprise
 — campaigns 83
simplicity vs minimalism
99–100
Skittles 41
story-telling *see* narratives
Style Guides 48–49, 61–62
surprise 27–39, 54
 — anticipation and 30, 34–35
 — attention 27, 28, 29, 34,
 37, 38
 — benefits
 — brain structure and
 function 29

 — curiosity and 30, 31
 — definition 30
 — effectiveness 36
 — effects of 27–29, 30–34
 — emotion and 32–33
 — engagement 28–29
 — examples 30, 31–32
 — expectations 28
 — influence 41, 54
 — learning 27, 30–31, 32
 — practical ideas 36–38
 — routine vs 32–33
 — shock vs 33–34, 38
 — timing 33–34, 37
 — tolerance for 32–33
superiority theory of
laughter 89
swearing 80
Swiss Army knife 95–96, 99

time scale 11
timing
 — shock 33–34, 38
 — surprise 37

Uber 128
unpredictability 15
unspoken language 151,
152–154

visual language 158–162,
175; *see also* visual sense and
approach
 — pros and cons 161
visual sense and approach
41–55
 — attention 41, 42, 43, 44, 46,
 47–48, 53, 54
 — attraction to moving objects
 44–45
 — benefits 41–43

visual *(Cont'd)*
- —bias towards 41–43
- —brain structure and function 41, 44
- —branding 48–50
- —branding, internal vs external 43, 48–49, 54
- —connection 42, 48
- —consistency 48–49, 54
- —curiosity 48
- —data, representing 45–57, 52
- —design 42
- —differentiation 47–50, 53
- —effects of 42–43
- —emotion and data 46
- —examples 43, 47, 49–50
- —habituation 48
- —learning 44
- —memory and recall 45
- —in narratives 74
- —practical ideas 51–54
- —recognition 43, 48, 54
- —surprise 48
- —using visuals 51
- —vs verbal 103–104

word choice 107–115; *see also* communication; language and perception; modes of delivery; visual language; names
- —abstract vs concrete language 111–112, 114
- —active vs passive voice 108–109
- —alignment 107
- —attention 108, 128–129
- —benefits 108
- —emotions, relationship with 78–81
- —familiar vs inclusive 112–113
- —formal vs colloquial 112, 114
- —importance of 114–115
- —inclusion vs exclusion 113, 145
- —indirect language 103
- —influence 101, 108, 109–110, 111, 112
- —jargon 49, 99, 102, 107, 112, 113, 115, 129, 134, 144, 168
- —loaded language 109–110, 114
- —organisational values 111
- —practical ideas 114–115
- —rhetorical vs relational language 110, 114
- —variation 113